Quality Teaching in a Culture of Coaching

Stephen G. Barkley
Terri Bianco, Contributing Editor

Rowman & Littlefield Education
Lanham • New York • Toronto • Oxford

Published in the United States of America
by Rowman & Littlefield Education
A Division of Rowman & Littlefield Publishers, Inc.
A wholly owned subsidiary of The Rowman & Littlefield Publishing Group, Inc.
4501 Forbes Boulevard, Suite 200, Lanham, Maryland 20706
www.rowmaneducation.com

PO Box 317
Oxford
OX2 9RU, UK

British Library Cataloguing in Publication Information Available

Library of Congress Cataloging-in-Publication Data

Barkley, Stephen G. (Stephen George), 1950–
   Quality teaching in a culture of coaching / Stephen G. Barkley; Terri
Bianco, contributing editor.
     p. cm.
   Includes bibliographical references and index.
   1. Teachers—In-service training. 2. Mentoring in education. 3.
Teachers—Professional relationships. I. Bianco, Terri.
II. Title

LB1731,B274 2005
370'.71'5—dc22   2004014855

ISBN-13: 978-1-57886-189-7 (pbk. : alk. paper)
ISBN-10: 1-57886-189-6 (pbk. : alk. paper)

♾™ The paper used in this publication meets the minimum requirements of
American National Standard for Information Sciences—Permanence of
Paper for Printed Library Materials, ANSI/NISO Z39.48-1992.
Manufactured in the United States of America.

Contents

PART III: APPLICATIONS OF COACHING

Foreword

Many daunting problems in education are borne of the isolation of teachers. Teaching requires the highest concentration of adults in the workplace of nearly any profession, and, ironically, it is the most isolating as well. There is no such thing as excellence in teaching when in solitude. By definition, excellence in teaching is a form of communication and group activity.

A coaching relationship contributes significantly to diminishing this isolation, particularly when the coaching involves experienced and expert practitioners sharing their knowledge and skills with more novice educators. There are national impulses in the direction of more collaboration among educators, yet the situation is changing much too slowly. In most schools, teachers are judged on their work as individuals. Policies and practices encourage individualism and do not sufficiently promote collective actions on the part of teachers. New teachers end up learning their job by "sink or swim."

Thus, it was with great relief and excitement that I learned Steve Barkley was authoring a book on the subject of coaching. Not only is Steve a highly skilled educator and presenter, but his focus on the empowerment of teachers has always been paramount. Rather than viewing teachers as targets for reforms, he equips them with the capacity to be agents of reform. His approach underscores the value of the synergy that comes when teacher and coach spend productive time reflecting, polishing, improving, and focusing their efforts on greater rewards for student and teacher alike.

Japan has long known the exponential benefit of coaching and teaching. While Japan's school year is the longest in the world, teachers' direct contact with students is less than in the United States. Japanese teachers devote half their work time to joint planning, sharing their lessons with other educators, conferring about students, and learning from each other. They call this "polishing the stone." American teachers should take example from this process and spend less time in frantic isolation and more time in thoughtful collaboration.

I envision a teacher union that acts not only as an advocate for educators but also as a lobby for all students. Coaching provides a piston for that effort. Steve Barkley played a vital role in bringing peer coaching into our teachers' negotiated contract as early as 1987. We believe in this direction so strongly that we have included peer coaching assistance, peer review, and now coaching and mentor programs in all our negotiated contracts.

These programs are hugely successful, but they may not have been so without the infrastructure of knowledge that Steve and Performance Learning Systems provided us. We have now leveraged those programs into new provisions that call for team transfers. Teachers no longer view themselves as individual practitioners; rather, they combine with other teachers—those who have been coached or are coaches in order to transfer into the same low-performing schools.

The distinguishing difference about Steve's approach is that he shares with a wider audience and with the educational community the work he has actually done, work he has honed over two decades. This is not a question of someone offering commentary on the work of others; this is someone exposing work formed by his own experience. A book written by a dynamic and skilled practitioner such as Steve is vastly more actionable, valuable, and pragmatic than one that only offers up theoretical speculation.

Steve's broad experience throughout the country and his knowledge about practices in other countries give him a basis for observing patterns and for commenting and for helping us avoid negative findings and false starts, wrong turns, pitfalls. This is wisdom gained from decades of experience about what to do and what not to do, what works and what doesn't. It's a huge bargain for readers to have all that concentrated for them so they can avoid the hard knocks involved in gaining direct experience on this critical theme.

Bravo, Steve. A book about coaching in teaching by an accomplished teacher coach is a book whose time has come.

Adam Urbanski, Ph.D.

Adam Urbanski is president of the Rochester Teachers Association, vice president of the American Federation of Teachers, and director of the Teacher Union Reform Network (TURN) of AFT and NEA Locals. A native of Poland, Dr. Urbanski immigrated at the age of fourteen. He earned a Ph.D. in American social history from the University of Rochester. A former high school teacher and college professor, Dr. Urbanski is an active proponent of change in education.

Acknowledgments

I would like to express my sincere appreciation and admiration to the team that helped develop this book.

Terri Bianco for her enthusiasm, support, and terrific writing and editing skills.

Miriam Georg, executive vice president for Product Development and creative director for Performance Learning Systems, Inc. (PLS), for her experience teaching coaching and supporting this book by seeing it through the proper channels.

Barbara Brown, chief editor of the Product Development team at PLS for her editing and efficiency in preparing the manuscript for the publisher.

Shari Resinger, Victor Printing, for making graphic sense of my scribblings.

Adam Urbanski, Ph.D., president of Rochester Teachers Association and vice president of American Federation of Teachers, for his continuing support, dedication, inspiration, and kind words.

Tom Koerner, Ph.D., publisher, and the staff of ScarecrowEducation for offering to publish this book.

To my early mentors, coaches, and peers in New Jersey and beyond who guided me as an educator, and to Joseph Hasenstab, founder of Performance Learning Systems, who trained me, inspired me, and encouraged me to bring knowledge, skills, performance, and heart to the profession of teaching.

With great appreciation to the following educators, coaches, and administrators who shared programs and experiences and contributed their thoughts to the context of this coaching book. Barbara Carroll, supervisor, teacher, and coach, Cranford High School, Cranford, New Jersey; Karen Bailin, teacher and coach, Cranford High School, Cranford, New Jersey; Joseph Corriero, Ed.D., Cranford board of education, Cranford, New Jersey; Mary Jo Scalzo, Ph.D., director of curriculum instruction and assessment, Oakwood City School District, Dayton, Ohio; Judy Hennessey, superintendent, Oakwood City School District, Dayton, Ohio; Debbie Smith, educator and coach, Oakwood City High School, Dayton, Ohio; Judy Sheehan, curriculum resource director, Winter Park Tech, Winter Park, Florida; Cheryl Jones, supervisor and reading first teacher and coach, School District of Hillsborough County, Daytona Beach, Florida; Cindy Petree, educator and coach, Stillwater High School, Stillwater, Oklahoma; Marilyn Katzenmeyer, Ed.D., leadership development coordinator, Tampa Bay Educational Leadership Collaborative, University of South Florida, Tampa, Florida; Jean Linder, Ph.D., University of South Florida, College of Education, Tampa, Florida; Sheryl Williams, reading coach, Alturas Elementary School, Alturas, Florida; Donna L. Behn, Ph.D., director of curriculum and instruction, Hartford Union High School, Hartford, Wisconsin; Dan Roskom, educator and lead coach, Hartford Union High School, Hartford, Wisconsin; Valerie Maxwell, math specialist, Appoquinimina School District, Middletown, Delaware; Hara Blum, reading specialist, Brandywine School District, Wilmington, Delaware.

Finally to all the teachers, coaches, principals, administrators, colleagues at PLS, and students who have shared their experiences and the benefits of coaching with me over the years. You have served as the inspiration and the motivation to create this book.

Many thanks to you all. Be sure to spread the word: Wow!

Introduction

I began teaching school in 1971 in an experimental student teaching program at East Stroudsburg State University in Pennsylvania. I taught a class of eighteen fourth graders. It was a kick. I loved it. What I didn't realize, however, was that I was truly blessed. For in that fourth-grade classroom I had a master teacher, another student teacher, and a graduate intern, all of whom supported and helped me.

I was essentially observed every day for 180 days. As soon as a lesson was completed, I received immediate feedback and encouragement. I also served as an observer for every other teacher in the school and did what most good teachers do—I stole as many of their ideas as I could!

When I took my first paid teaching position the following year in an Individual Guided Education (IGE) school in New Jersey, there was always someone around to see or hear what I was telling the students. Colleagues were present to help brainstorm possible strategies for learning.

After teaching fourth, fifth, and sixth graders for several years, I transferred to a first-grade class. I survived my first year of teaching first grade only because I was teamed with an experienced teacher who coached me through the process. Without her support, feedback, questions, and acknowledgment, I may not have succeeded in that first year.

One of the things I learned during that time was the value of celebrating success among teachers. Here's how it happened. In that first-grade classroom, I discovered that learning to read is a miracle. Students could go home on a Wednesday unable to read and miraculously come back Thursday morning reading!

But one student—little Mikey—was just not learning how to read. I was concerned as the end of year approached that he would not succeed before summer. Since I had developed a collegial relationship with all the other teachers in the school, I asked for help. I tried all their ideas, including those from special education teachers and reading consultants.

In late May, it happened. Mikey read. I ran around the school proclaiming, "Mikey learned to read today! He did it! He read!" It was then that I learned I was working with a faculty that understood the need to celebrate. The next afternoon, a group of teachers walked into my classroom with a cheese ball and a bottle of champagne, and we celebrated Mikey's learning to read.

Providing teachers with opportunities to celebrate is one of the key benefits of coaching. Coaching also provides opportunities for teachers to add to their lesson plans and techniques—their repertoire, if you will. Coaching also offers teachers the opportunity to undertake some *conscious* practicing of their techniques, strategies, and the various moves of teaching.

I eventually left teaching children to become an instructor at Performance Learning Systems, providers of graduate courses for teachers. I have been training teachers, principals, administrators, and staff for over twenty-five years. From the beginning, I benefited from coaching. As an instructor, I was videotaped countless times. I scrutinized my performance patterns and teaching techniques, and others scrutinized them along with me. Ego had to take a back seat as the importance of delivering instruction took precedence.

As a presenter, I am often videotaped, both to develop a teaching product and also for others to review. Certainly that would not have been possible without the coaching and invaluable feedback from the videotapes. Working with school districts, state departments of education, educational associations, and conferences around the country, I sensed an almost complete absence of opportunities for teachers to receive actual feedback on how they teach. So often, they are not coached on the specific practices they undertake to achieve learning in their students, despite research that points resoundingly to the power of coaching in teacher performance. I realized the tremendous gift of coaching I had received earlier in my career.

We have filmed and videotaped basketball games to help improve the players' performances for over fifty years. Yet there are a scant number of teachers who have ever had their lessons videotaped. Imagine having a library of videotapes with teachers teaching various subjects at different grades levels using highly creative techniques, all available to other teachers—both new teachers and seasoned teachers. These tapes—or digital discs—would not only capture the creative and effective lesson plan but provide viewers with motivation, ideas, inspiration, and professional improvement.

We are all aware of the major changes that have occurred in education because of the vast amount of information and technology coming our way and also because of the broadened scope of a teacher's and an administrator's swath of responsibility. The job has gone way beyond spouting data in hopes students will receive it. Teachers are educators, social workers, caregivers, nutritionists, disciplinarians, paralegals, paperpushers, parent advisors, as well as nose-blowers. They need all the support they can get.

I have experienced the tremendous boost a culture of coaching provides these professional educators. I am heartened by the personal and professional benefits it provides not only for these educators but ultimately for their students, who enjoy a heightened passion on the part of their teachers. Coached teachers are fiercely self-aware about their practice. They reflect on how they achieve learning in their students; other professionals who desire that they succeed support them.

This book promises to provide a framework for you as a professional educator or administrator to incorporate a culture of coaching into your own educational environment. It outlines the why, who, what, and how of a sound coaching program. I have included concrete examples, opportunities to practice specific skills, a clearly defined coaching process, coaching applications for a wide array of school professionals, and real-life anecdotes and quotes to pepper it all up.

I hope this book will both inspire you to continue or initiate a coaching program and that it will serve as a resource as you implement and build your own coaching program.

I

THE VALUE OF COACHING

1

Why Coaching?

When Stillwater, Oklahoma, teacher Cindy Petree attended her first coaching class, she took a deep breath, swallowed, and admitted to other teachers gathered there that she wished she were as good a teacher working on her own as she was when she knew someone was watching her. To her surprise, others shared they often felt exactly the same way. Cindy knew then that peer coaching was about to become a big part of her life.

At Winter Park Tech in Orange County, Florida, teachers and administrators decided to work together to improve everyone's professional abilities. The thirty-minute sessions took place after school and covered topics such as classroom management, communication, presentation skills, team-building activities, use of peer evaluations, and student motivation techniques.

Winter Park Curriculum Resource Director Judy Sheehan says, "This coaching process opened lines of communication. We really *talked* to one another. We're not just broad-brushing our feedback by saying, 'Oh, you did fine' or 'That was nice.' We gave specific feedback to teachers and administrators always focusing on their specific needs and challenges."

The Oakwood City School District in Ohio began a coaching program with fifty staff members and nine administrators. It has since grown to encompass nearly a third of the school teaching population, with plans to continue the program until all teachers and administrators have been trained.

"Our district's philosophy is to include job-embedded professional development wherever possible," says Dr. Mary Jo Scalzo, Director of Curriculum, Instruction and Assessment at Oakwood. "This is critical because teachers are working with one another on technical practice in the classroom. With coaching, there's someone there for them. The process always focuses on the teacher being coached."

Success stories such as these abound across the country. Coaching has proven to be one of the primary tools of staff development for teachers and administrators alike. Coaching provides a vehicle by which to achieve goals, improve strategies, and make a difference for students and colleagues. With coaching, teachers discover—usually for the first time—how to reflect on their teaching in ways that add value to their methods and an enhanced level of professionalism. They see and hear themselves as educators. They get opportunities for receiving direct feedback on how they have interacted with their students. They increase their ability to design lesson plans that focus on specific strategies they want to implement to reach *all* their students.

The resulting support and feedback from colleagues has a bonus effect—teachers at the same school develop a synergy of creativity. When administrators and teachers together undertake a coaching program, it gets even better. Schoolwide collegial support develops. Students receive the benefit of an improved teacher in their classrooms; administrators receive the respect and support from an admiring and productive staff. All receive the caring and support for each other. A quality learning experience occurs for students and throughout the learning community.

THE GIFT OF COACHING

But why coaching? How does coaching create this synergy, this support, and these successes? Let's start by saying what it's not. Coaching is not about fixing someone. No one is broken, and no one needs fixing. It's not about giving advice, providing "constructive criticism," making judgment, or providing an opinion.

Coaching is a relationship between two equals, one of whom is committed to making personal and professional improvements. These improvements may come in the form of wanting to learn new strategies, to get unblocked or unstuck, to reevaluate beliefs or values affecting professional outlook. It could be to look at habits or change strategies. Whatever it is, the person being coached—the coachee—takes ownership of his or her own improvement. Therein lies its power.

Each person being coached is committed to his or her own achievements. Those being coached know what it is they need to work on, and thus there is relevancy and consequence to doing the work, achieving the goal, succeeding. In committing to coaching, they commit to their well-being and skill as professional educators.

A coaching relationship provides the opportunity for reciprocity of gifts of knowledge and skill, caring and support, feedback and celebration. In the coaching relationship, people being coached are the ones in charge. They are in charge because they have the agenda, the commitment, and the specifics of what they want to know or learn about their skills as a professional. Nothing gets discussed that the coachee does not want to discuss. The relationship is focused on achieving the results desired by the coachee.

The coach, in turn, ensures that the coachee always steers toward the goal, the achievement, the fulfillment, and the success. Sometimes the coachee has questions he or she wants to explore. Otherwise, the coach asks the questions; the person being coached usually has the answers when given a forum to discover them for him- or herself.

Yet as the person being coached goes through the process of coaching, the coach achieves his or her own level of success. Imagine how the coach must feel when the teacher being coached exclaims that the goal was reached or that the process, strategy, or lesson plan really worked. Feedback received from the coach served as "feedforward," moving the teacher or administrator along in a way that achieved success. The coach reaps rewards when the coachee excels.

A culture of coaching improves teaching and improves student learning. Teachers once entered a classroom, closed the door, and taught primarily on their own, doing the best they could, relying on their years of education and experience. They were there to impart knowledge and see that learning occurred. Those days are long gone. Teachers are now not only charged with helping students learn in a world drowning in new information and technology but are called upon to serve as social worker, nutritionist, counselor, whistle-blower, cop, nose-blower, and more.

We all know teaching has changed. Like all other professions, the need for support from colleagues, coaches, and mentors is long overdue. We pay athletes, performers, television personalities, business executives, and other professionals millions of dollars to perform with quality, effectiveness, and assurance. Each of these professions has an array of coaches, in one form or another, providing what the coachee needs.

Teaching is no different. In fact, it is more important that educators receive support to do their very, very best. After all, there are children's futures at stake.

COACHING WORKS

Research shows that teachers' skill development markedly increases when opportunities for practice and feedback are provided. To be maximally useful, such feedback must be both specific and descriptive. The addition of coaching to teachers' staff development greatly enhances their implementation of skills in class.

Educational researchers Bruce Joyce and Beverly Showers in their book *Student Achievement through Staff Development* point out that staff development training often assumes that once teachers learn and develop a skill, they will automatically use it in the classroom. Yet their research reveals it isn't a sure thing that learned knowledge and skills will transfer. However, you can expect to have a noticeable increase in transfer when coaching is added to a teacher's training.

Training or coaching that provides transfer of skills into instructional settings is crucial for learning. The table 1.1, Transfer of Learning by Types of Training, developed by Joyce and Showers, illustrates the increased transfer of learning when a coaching component is added.

Table 1.1. Transfer of Learning by Types of Training

Training Provided	Skill Development	Accurate Use in Class
Theory/Knowledge	5%	0 to 5%
Theory/Modeling	50%	5%
Theory/Modeling/ Practice/Feedback	90%	5%
Theory/Modeling/ Practice/Feedback/ Coaching	90%	75 to 90%

Source: *The Coaching of Teaching* by Joyce and Showers 1993.

This table shows a relationship among types of training and the percentage of participants who will accurately use a developed skill and achieve a desired outcome.

Figure 1.1 shows the five steps that take place for internalization of learning, according to Joyce and Showers.

Joyce and Showers consider *knowledge* the awareness of educational theories and practices, new curricula, or academic content. It includes the exploration of theory or rationale through reading, lectures, and discussion. An outcome has been achieved when the knowledge—awareness—has been achieved.

Figure 1.1.   Learning a Skill

Modeling demonstrates discrete behaviors and skills; *practice* includes implementation of those behaviors or skills, such as the ability to deliver questions, use pause time, engage students through eye contact and inquiry, etc. *Observation* occurs in the coaching process, as does *feedback*.

The reality of teaching in a classroom, of course, is vastly different from a training session where teachers learn and even practice new skills or techniques. According to Joyce and Showers, while practicing skills will certainly increase their use in the classroom, coaching and feedback provide the most significant leap in transfer of learning for the one being coached. Learning teaching practices presented in training is highly valuable, but unless teachers can deliver the skills in the classroom, outside a training session, there's little chance they will continue to use the skills among their daily teaching strategies. A separate, metacognitive learning experience eventually transfers to teaching behavior patterns that are natural and effective.

Beyond transfer, the feedback provided by coaching is extremely beneficial to the teacher. Coaches can see confusion or omissions when watching other people teach more easily than they can recognize it in themselves. Therefore, they learn in the process too.

Other research findings underscore the value of a peer coaching relationship:

- The ultimate goal of any staff development effort is the transfer of the new learning to the teacher's active repertoire (Joyce & Showers 2003).
- What new teachers want in their induction programs are "experienced colleagues who will take their daily dilemmas seriously, watch them teach and provide feedback, help them teach and provide feedback, help them develop instructional strategies, model skilled teaching, and share insights about students' work" (Johnson & Kardos 2002).
- Following peer coaching, teachers report substantial increase in the use of skills and strategies to support instructional change (Bowman & McCormick 2000; Doughtery 1993; Kohler, Crilley, Shearer, & Good 1997; Wineburg 1995).
- Joyce and Showers (1990) reported that 80 percent of the teachers who had received coaching implemented new strategies, versus only 10 percent of the teachers who received instruction without follow-up coaching.

- Collegial self-reflection—in which teachers are trained in observation, interview, and analysis skills and then observe and write portraits of each others' teaching—increases teachers' self-awareness, critical thinking, collegiality, and interdisciplinary teaching (Harriman 1992).
- Jenkins and Veal (2002) conclude that benefits accrued far outweigh the additional time required for coaching of beginning teachers.
- Teachers rate learning from other teachers second only to their own teaching experiences as the most valuable source of information about effective teaching (Smylie 1989).
- Teachers value learning from their colleagues more than from university professors, administrators, consultants, or specialists (Morrison et al. 1994; Raney & Robbins 1989; Smylie 1989).
- Teachers who received peer coaching after attending training workshops increased use of specific skills more than did teachers who only attended workshops (Heberly 1991).
- Teachers who completed an eight-week training program but received no coaching reported positive attitudes toward the training and intentions to implement the content in their classrooms. Yet, in a follow-up study, those teachers who were not coached had discontinued use of the practices and had difficulty demonstrating the competencies taught in the training program (Baker 1983).
- The coaching relationship results in the possibility of mutual reflecting, the checking of perceptions, the sharing of frustrations and successes, and informal thinking through of mutual problems (Joyce & Showers 1982).

Let's be real. Coaching goes on all the time anyway. Teachers in supportive relationships with others constantly reinforce one another. Teachers share confusion over new standards with one another, they support each other in complex lesson planning, and they are there for one another when discipline problems crop up.

While teachers and administrators use conferences and meetings to get ideas and support from fellow professionals, the more common form is from one another. Teachers seek out teachers for support and administrators seek out administrators for support—and the operative word here is "support."

The human need to share, to improve, to seek help is ever present, even in the hectic schedule of an educator. Why not capitalize on the need by following a process destined to improve the quality of teaching and learning? Coaching invites diversity of style and of approach. It improves teaching, confidence, and raises the bar on professionalism.

HAROLD, QUALITY, AND THE EMERALD BUS

Improving the quality of life for teachers improves the quality of life for students and thus the quality of learning. A quote I like to use, because it defines quality for me, is from William Glasser, M.D., author of *Choice Theory, The Quality School, The Quality School Teacher,* and *Choice Theory in the Classroom.* In his article "Quality, Trust, and Redefining Education," Glasser (1992) says:

> While quality is difficult to define precisely, it almost always includes caring for each other, is always useful, has always involved hard work on someone's part, and when we are involved with it, as either a provider or a receiver, it always feels good. Because it feels so good, I believe all of us carry in our heads a clear idea of what quality is for ourselves.

I like his description, as I can immediately identify quality as I work in school districts around the country. Quality is visible not only in a school's environment; it is apparent in the way students and teachers interact, in the excitement of the students, in the faces of teachers and administrators, and in the teamwork of the staff.

We often speak of quality products and quality service in the consumer world, but what about quality experiences in teaching and learning? As an educator, parent, or administrator, don't you want to work in an environment where quality happens, where you know quality is achieved, both in teaching and learning?

When I speak to various groups, I often share the following incident that underscores the value of a quality experience. It identifies in a concrete way the components of Glasser's quote about quality. It goes like this:

I arrived at the Atlanta airport on a Sunday night. It was late. My plane had been delayed, and I still had to rent a car and drive to a hotel near the school where I was presenting the following day. I was tired, and as I took the tram and then the escalator from the plane to the terminal, a huge line of people waiting to rent cars was there ahead of me. Discouraged and resigned, I moved to the end of the line.

After a few moments, I noticed a sign on the wall over a computer. It said "Welcome Emerald Plus Cardholders." I recalled I had an Emerald Plus card. It was bright green, and I found it immediately in my wallet. While this was in my "early computer" days, I nevertheless went up to the computer, saw a slot about the size of my green plastic card and popped it in. Boom! Up on the screen appeared the words "Welcome to Atlanta, Stephen G. Barkley!" I sheepishly looked back at the line, slightly embarrassed that someone might have seen this.

Beneath that greeting were two words: "Rent" and "Return." I clicked on "Rent," and up came another screen showing pictures of four cars. I picked the red Corsica, and out dropped a set of keys and a printed rental agreement! Feeling very cocky but trying not to show it, I sauntered past the long line of people, jingling my keys ever so slightly.

I went outside to catch the bus to the car rental lot and saw a big green bus pulling away. I waved, and to my surprise, the driver turned the bus around and came back to get me. He jumped out of the bus and grabbed two of my bags; I took the other two, showed him my keys and my rental agreement, climbed aboard, and plopped down, relieved.

Next the driver picked up the bus intercom and began speaking. Now, it's one o'clock in the morning, I'm the only person on the bus, and he says in a booming voice, "Welcome to Atlanta, Mr. Barkley. I'm Harold, your Emerald Flyer for the day!" Arriving at the parking lot, he unloaded my two bags. I got the other two, and he approached me and said, "Your keys are in the trunk. Your rental agreement is on the dashboard. Have a *wonderful* stay in Atlanta."

Wow. I realized then that I had more energy at one o'clock in the morning than I had had three hours before. That energy came from the *quality* in the experience.

Looking at Glasser's quote, he identifies four ways an experience represents quality. It includes *caring* for others. Certainly Harold showed that he cared. I can attest to the fact that helping with luggage is not in the typical job description of a rental-car bus driver.

Next, the experience was *useful*. The computer network system that generated a set of keys and a rental agreement was extremely useful to me. It meant I could get on my way sooner, get more sleep, and be more alert in my presentation to educators and administrators the following day.

Harold *worked hard*, as did the folks who made sure when I got to the parking lot there actually was a clean red Corsica there, the keys fit the car, and everything ran as it should. That takes hard work on the part of a large number of people.

Finally, and probably the most telling trait of quality—it *felt good*. It felt good for the provider and the recipient, for Harold and for me.

Coaching adds quality. It adds quality to the level of teaching as well as to the school environment. It shows *caring* on the part of the coach—he or she cares that the teacher or administrator succeeds. It is *useful*, as it adds quality to teaching and to student learning. It takes *hard work* to change, practice new skills or strategies, commit to improvement, get feedback, and recommit. And it *feels good*. It feels good to improve, to change, and to succeed; it feels good to have someone in your corner, coaching you to high achievement.

We'll work with some of Glasser's theories in chapter 3. For now, let's look at the idea of quality when considering a coaching program at your school or district. Begin with the idea of adding coaching to your life by asking questions about quality. Ask where the quality is in your school, your faculty relationships, and your interaction with students—and build on that.

Look to coaching to make it easier to have a school that's caring, to make it useful, and to set up an environment where hard work feels good. Quality circumstances produce positive energy. Quality permeates the school system—how the cafeteria works, the moods of educators, the productivity of students, the look of the hallways.

GETTING TO WOW

Quality means going "above and beyond" the norm. I learned about a teacher who gave out Cs to those students who completed a project successfully. To get a B they had to go beyond the project; to receive an A they needed to go above and beyond. Doing what's required is not quality. In any job, you don't get promoted for doing what you are asked to do. You don't get promoted for washing the dishes if you're a dishwasher. You get promoted if you wash the dishes and also polish the sink.

Peer coaching and working collaboratively with colleagues greatly improves the chances of going above and beyond the rote elements of teaching and into a realm about which Tom Peters writes in *The Pursuit of WOW!*

Achieving wow, to me, is achieving quality. Ask yourself: When does a student achieve a wow? On how many Fridays can a teacher add up the wows he or she received from students? Also, wows do not necessarily come from an entertaining presentation or activity. They are not entertainment. They are experiences of quality when a student feels exhilarated by a learning situation. How many opening days of school have wow quality—for students or for teachers?

Some opening-day wows I have witnessed include teachers who dress in costume to represent historical characters for history class. Or they come as the main character of the first book students have to read in English.

A math teacher brought single dollar bills to school on opening day and handed them out to each student. He told them if they passed math, they could keep the dollar. If they didn't pass, they had to return the dollar— with interest compounded daily! You can bet they learned about interest very quickly.

A special-education teacher in Georgia learned her class would be held that year in a portable trailer. The first day of school she dressed with curlers in her hair, slippers on her feet, and licorice on her teeth to look like they were missing—making the point they were located in a trailer, away from the main school building. After a few minutes of students gawking at her, she disrobed and underneath had on a beautiful sequined dress, high heels, and classy jewelry. She told the children that their trailer was like Cinderella's magic pumpkin. All sorts of magic occurred there, and they were going to have a year of wonderful, magical surprises.

If teachers wow kids, someone has to wow teachers now and then, too. The need for excitement and motivation that applies to students presumably also applies to teachers—maybe even more so. Teachers typically start school going over classroom rules, because administrators start their year with rules for teachers and students. Administrators talk about "have tos" instead of "going tos": "We have to meet standards this year"; "We have to make up for last year's snow days"; "We have to provide more discipline."

Imagine the quality that would result in telling teachers, "We're going to have a great year!" "We're planning an exciting parent-teacher day." "We're going to get a new computer network system." "We're going to have a lot of fun this year!" "We're going to give you support by providing you with a professional coaching program this year."

Coaching introduces quality to a relationship. Because coaches support the success of teachers—just as teachers support the success of their students—teachers gain the experience of having someone in their corner rooting for them. That's a quality feeling. Wow!

THREE OUTCOMES OF COACHING

Embedded within the coaching process are three outcomes that are enjoyed by the person being coached—the teacher.

Celebrations

The first outcome of coaching is Celebration. Celebrations are opportunities to give colleagues recognition. This recognition adds quality to a teacher's life. This is their chance to have a "wow" experience.

Examples of Celebrations

Here are some opening-day celebrations or "wowers" I've heard about from teachers. One principal rented a red carpet and invited the parents of students to come on the first day of school. The teachers walked into the school along the red carpet as the principal, students, and parents applauded them.

Another principal provided coffee and donuts at a local racetrack. The principal wanted to accelerate learning, so he had the owner bring out some race cars and took the teachers on a lap or two at high-speed acceleration. They got the point—quickly.

At a high school in Florida, football players each picked a teacher they wanted to honor. During a home game, the players wore their regular home uniforms, and the teachers each wore the "away" uniform of the player who had picked them. Number 48 on the halfback corresponded to number 48 on Mrs. McGyver's jersey. The teachers jogged out onto the field behind the players, to the applause of the fans and the team.

The point is that these simple, inexpensive wow events create quality. They generate motivation and excitement. They celebrate the profession of educators.

But every day cannot be an opening day at school. That's where coaching comes in. A key component of any coaching program is celebration. Achievement, improvement, and success need the closure of a celebration to lock in the success, show caring and support, reward the hard work, and, of course, to feel good. Celebration says the coaching process works. The coach celebrates the coachee's ability to set up a goal and fulfill it. The coachee acknowledges the coach's support by his or her very success.

Options

The second outcome of coaching is Options. Who are the greatest teachers? The greatest teachers are those with the longest list of options at their disposal. They are not great teachers because they know what to do. They are great teachers because they always have something else to try. They never give up. If one thing doesn't work, they try something else.

Teachers don't always know what is going to work in a given situation. Instead, they have a long list of strategies from which to choose. They are always experimenting. Being a great teacher means you don't run out of experiments before the year is over.

Coaches can provide the feedback on strategies or experiments tried as well as help the teacher brainstorm new strategies, new options. In fact, coaching can greatly reduce a teacher's stress. As coach and coachee confer, interact, and develop mutual support and trust, more options are discovered, alleviating the stress of not knowing what to do next.

Conscious Practice

The third outcome of a coaching program is Conscious Practice. As we shall see in chapter 3, learning a new strategy or skill takes one through various steps of achievement. As teachers try different techniques, they

are given opportunities with a supportive coach to practice those techniques consciously, without fear of reprisal. They practice in a safe, trusting environment. This not only provides more confidence but underscores
the value of more options available to practice.

THREE KINDS OF COACHING

All coaching is geared toward a specific goal, whether skills-based, the-
ory-based, behavioral, or attitudinal. Robert J. Garmston, in his article
"How Administrators Support Peer Coaching" (1987), identifies three different coaching approaches. The approach used depends on the ultimate
result desired. Garmston has called these three approaches Technical
Coaching, Collegial Coaching, and Challenge Coaching.

Technical Coaching

Technical Coaching is said to assist teachers in applying their staff-
development training in the classroom. It relies on the concept that objective feedback can improve teaching performance. Technical coaching is
generally given following staff-development workshops on specific
teaching methods, such as learning styles or cooperative learning.

Its intent is to impart a specific strategy the teacher can apply immediately in the classroom. While this approach has tremendous value in that regard, it has a few problems. Foremost is the perception among those being
coached that this process is more like an evaluation than a coaching session.

Whether the specific strategy or behavior shows up in the classroom is
often recorded on assessment forms. The form may judge the practice to
have occurred "thoroughly," "partially," "missing," or as having been "not
needed"—giving the air of a formal evaluation. The process also lends itself to coaches' giving their coachees unsolicited "advice" that can lead to
defensiveness on the part of the person being told what to do or how to do
it. To succeed, technical coaching requires accurate, specific feedback
about the technical strategy being coached. If a staff-development workshop was on the use of pause time when asking questions, for example,
the technical coaching approach would be to look for how the teacher applied pause time—that and only that.

Challenge Coaching

Challenge Coaching involves a group effort. A team forms to resolve specific and ongoing problems—thus the word "challenge." Unlike other forms of coaching, the team may consist of noneducators called in to provide their perspectives and expertise to help resolve a problem. This team approach in a coaching environment requires mutual trust among colleagues as they focus on solving the problem together, whether in the curriculum, instructional techniques, logistics, school structure, classroom management, or any other persistent issue.

The challenge coaching process begins with the identification of the problem. An example might be a group of fifth-grade teachers concerned about the amount of homework required and time needed to grade papers. Small groups of coaches and the fifth-grade teachers facing the problem meet to brainstorm solutions and develop action plans. The group may explore staggering assignments, for example, or teaming up on grading. Unlike technical coaching and collegial coaching (below), which include one-on-one interaction, challenge coaching consists of a group working together to deal with the problem.

Collegial Coaching

Collegial Coaching focuses on giving teachers time and support to think metacognitively about their work in a safe atmosphere with plenty of support. Its intent is to improve teaching practices, enhance relationships with colleagues, and increase professional communication about teaching practices. The underlying notion—backed by research—is that a teacher will acquire and deepen teaching strategies, habits, and reflection about his or her teaching when given an opportunity to develop and practice these skills with feedback from peers.

Collegial coaching usually includes a dyad of teacher-to-teacher, administrator-to-teacher, administrator-to-administrator, or other pair. The person being observed names the specific focus of the coaching desired—a specific technique to practice or a behavior to correct. The coach observes both the teacher and the students in the classroom, gathering the data he or she needs to give objective and specific feedback.

While a technical coach may judge a teacher's performance, the collegial coach helps the teacher analyze, interpret, and judge for him- or herself how decisions affecting student learning and professional achievement were met.

The collegial coaching process is the focus of this book.

TIGER WOODS AND TWO COACHING BELIEFS

Two beliefs can build a successful coaching culture:

Belief No. 1: Everyone working in a school should be observed once a week and receive feedback.

Belief No. 2: The most skilled and professional educators should receive the most coaching.

Why would we have a belief like number two? Simple. It generates more options for teachers that are already good or great.

The farther up the ladder of success one goes, the more coaching is needed. It's what I call the Tiger Woods syndrome. Tiger had only his dad as a coach when he first started playing golf. Now he needs multiple coaches. As he gets better, he needs to improve even more until he becomes the best. As he achieves success, he needs to achieve more. He needs coaches to improve his swing, and he probably also needs coaches to help him deal with fame and success. He most assuredly needs a financial coach!

The most skilled and professional educator in a school can serve as a role model for others. This person models for others the ideas that

- constant improvement is part of the profession;
- it's okay to be coached as a successful professional;
- coaching is an opportunity to learn new strategies, to come up with creative lesson plans, to increase one's bag of tricks, so to speak, in order to avoid falling into the rut of doing the same things year after year;
- coaching doesn't mean you need fixing. You're not broken. You just want to improve and get better at what you do;
- you gain a solid return on the investment of teacher education by learning every day better ways to teach.

Providing coaching to even the most skilled professionals not only allows those professionals to improve but gives them recognition—someone cares. Skilled professionals—great teachers—need acknowledgment and recognition. In many vocations, the more you do, the more you're ignored. You are taken for granted. Good people—great people—need recognition too.

GOOD TO GREAT

We will explore the differences between mentoring and coaching in chapter 2. It is my firm belief, however, that schools should not engage in a mentoring program unless they also have a coaching program in place. A mentoring program is usually developed to assist new teachers to come aboard, learn the ropes, and improve what they do. A coaching program, in contrast, can be applied to new teachers, tenured teachers, and anyone in between.

Good teachers benefit from coaching, as well as beginning teachers and those who are struggling. Good teachers want to be great teachers, and coaching provides them an avenue to become great teachers.

In the coaching process, teachers are observed once a week. Beyond observation, good teachers should be videotaped once a week. Yes, the coach can provide specific feedback from the observation, but nothing beats seeing and hearing yourself in action for focusing on techniques you definitely want to enhance and those you should leave on the cutting-room floor.

The combination of coaching and videotaping is powerful, because often teachers' very effectiveness can get in their way. They may have an excellent lesson plan; they are good at delivering it. Yet without an observer—a coach or a video camera—the teacher may never stop to ask whether the activity was worth the time the teacher and the students spent on it. Maybe the content wasn't worth saving. Maybe the activity was fun, but so what? Was it worth the effort?

When good coaches observe good teachers, synergy causes improvement to develop exponentially. Each builds on the other's input and desire to instill learning in students. The coach keeps the teacher focused on the outcome desired. The coach understands the teacher's thinking, because they have interacted in their conferences and interviews. The teacher is already a good teacher, and the coach is there to help make improvements, just as Tiger Woods is a good—a great—golfer coached regularly to keep him that way or make him even better.

The problem is not that we do not have enough good teachers. The problem is we have way too many. There is too much "good teaching." This good teaching has become totally acceptable, and some teachers have been doing this same good job for years. Good has become marginalized. To create a major improvement in learning within a system or a district or even a state, we need programs that will move large numbers of good teachers to become *great* teachers.

We are always talking about improving student performance. We want them to exert more effort. We say they have the potential if only they'd "apply" themselves. Yet isn't the same true for teachers—for all humans, really? Once we achieve a certain level of knowledge or skill, we tend to use it over and over, staying within our comfort zone. Learning more skills is a skill in and of itself.

Rafe Esquith (2003), winner of the American Teacher Award, inspires and challenges us to rethink the way we educate our children in his award-winning book *There Are No Shortcuts*. He cites a poem given him by Charles Osgood of CBS News. It goes like this:

Pretty Good
There once was a pretty good student,
Who sat in a pretty good class;
Who was taught by a pretty good teacher,
Who always let pretty good pass—
He wasn't terrific at reading,
He wasn't a whiz bang at math;
But for him education was leading
Straight down a pretty good path.
He didn't find school too exciting,
But he wanted to do pretty well;
And he did have some trouble with writing,
And no one had taught him to spell.
When doing arithmetic problems,
Pretty good was regarded as fine—
5 plus 5 needn't always add up to be 10,

A pretty good answer was 9.
The pretty good class that he sat in
Was part of a pretty good school;
And the student was not the exception,
On the contrary, he was the rule.
The pretty good student, in fact, was
Part of a pretty good mob;
And the first time he knew that he lacked was
When he looked for a pretty good job.
It was then, when he sought a position,
He discovered that life could be tough—
And he soon had a sneaking suspicion,
Pretty good might not be good enough.
The pretty good town in our story
Was part of a pretty good state,
Which had pretty good aspirations,
And prayed for a pretty good fate.
There once was a pretty good nation,
Pretty proud of the greatness it had,
Which learned much too late, if you want to be great,
Pretty good is, in fact, pretty bad. (p. 55)

Coaching can move good teachers to become great teachers. It provides the strongest return on the investment of teaching. Coaches may cause discomfort at times. However, great coaches create environments where the coachee is comfortable with discomfort. Discomfort is key to growth and change. When good teachers become uncomfortable, that discomfort gives them impetus to improve, to wake up and get out of their box; it stimulates positive change. Coaching only struggling teachers misses the point of who could be coached, and it often eliminates the opportunity to coach good teachers to greatness.

SUMMARY

As we will see in chapter 2, coaching takes on many forms. Its applications are endless. What I want to convey here is the true value of coaching—that it creates quality. It moves teachers from good to great. While technical and challenge coaching have their place, collegial coaching provides a connection that results in creative synergy. In addition, collegial coaching often leads to technical or challenge coaching as an outgrowth of the process. Research is solid in its support of coaching's effectiveness in teacher improvement. Coaching provides opportunities for teachers to practice their profession consciously. It increases their options, and it affords them opportunities to celebrate, locking in their achievements, goals, and successes.

Isn't it nice to know a process that includes celebrations is an important, effective, and valuable part of quality teaching?

2

Who's on First? Defining the Role of the Coach

Peer coach, mentor, protégé, principal, evaluator, supervisor, curriculum coordinator, educator, administrator, union representative, director of staff development, site-based administrator, reading coach, chief academic officer—who *are* all these people? Academia is awash with titles and programs, and while titles vary from district to district, certain roles are similar in their purpose, function, and intent.

The primary distinction I want to make is among the roles of coach, mentor, supervisor, and evaluator as shown on the continuum in figure 2.1.

COACHING AND MENTORING: TWO DIFFERENT ROLES

The terms "coach" and "mentor" are often used interchangeably, yet the person in each role takes a different approach and has a different intent in similar situations. Mentors typically have a certain level of expertise and are assigned to assist someone ostensibly with less knowledge or experience. This person is like a protégé to the mentor, which Webster's defines as "a person guided and helped, especially in the furtherance of his or her career, by another, more influential person." A mentoring relationship can be one between an executive who takes an entry-level manager under his wing, or it can be a tenured educator assigned to a beginning teacher.

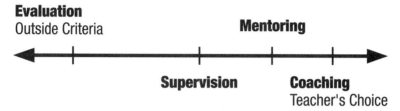

Figure 2.1.   Evaluation/Coaching Continuum

A "beginning" teacher may be someone who recently graduated, or an individual with teaching experience who is new to a state or district. It might be a teacher who has an assignment in a new department or a teacher experiencing difficulties and in need of additional support. In any case, the role of mentors is to guide, teach, tutor, and help mentees—showing them the ropes and imparting their own knowledge and experience.

The term "mentor" comes from Homer's *Odyssey.* Odysseus, king of Ithaca, went off for ten years to fight the Trojan War. While he was gone, he entrusted the care of his household and his son Telemachus to Mentor, who was a teacher and overseer of Telemachus—like a long-term babysitter and tutor. Eventually Telemachus and his father were reunited, and Mentor's reward was that his name has come to mean a trusted advisor, teacher, and wise person.

Mentor has now gone from Homer to the homeroom, as many school districts have in place mentoring programs, with participation often mandatory for beginning teachers. A mentoring program usually outlines specific tasks for the mentor. Mentors may be charged with providing knowledge about how the district works. They might be technology mentors or mentors for curriculum-oriented issues. Some help with moral development and others with technical competence.

A coach may do some of those tasks as well. Yet the primary difference is that a coach is usually someone *chosen by the one who wants to be coached.* There need not be a difference in abilities, skill, or knowledge between the two. A tenured teacher can coach a tenured colleague; teachers coach administrators and vice versa. Administrators can coach principals and vice versa. Coaching tends to be more empowering and stems from a partnership of support and development.

To me, the difference between mentor and coach can be equated to the semantic difference between the words "help" and "assist." *Helping* implies that someone cannot fare well alone, that outside help is needed to succeed or come up to speed. *Assisting* someone implies that the person is quite capable but needs assistance to pull together a skill, knowledge, or behavior. Coaching acknowledges one's capabilities. It empowers one to bring strengths to fruition. Its focus is on the "good to great" model described in chapter 1. It says, "You have strengths; let's discover them and fine-tune them, get them out into the classroom."

Mentoring, while also empowering a person to achieve, assumes something is lacking that needs to be fixed. As a deficit model, mentoring asks you to turn to your mentor when there's trouble. Schools assign mentors to beginning teachers because it's likely that they will need to iron out problems or will otherwise need help.

In many districts mentors work with beginning teachers only for a limited time. A new teacher comes into a school and is assigned a mentor. The mentor shows the teacher the ropes, then usually leaves the teacher alone. When the beginning teacher feels comfortable in the teaching role, the mentor disappears. If in the future the teacher needs some input or has trouble for some reason, in the future, a new mentor—or possibly a coach—is called in, implying that the teacher is now doing something *wrong* and needs the "help."

Mentoring is highly useful for teacher orientation, and mentors have been instrumental in helping new and beginning teachers familiarize themselves with what's expected of them, how things work. They increase the competence of beginning teachers so that they become a part of the professional staff; mentoring truly works in that regard. But what happens then? I believe that mentoring should segue into peer coaching—that a school or district should not have a mentoring program without a commensurate coaching program in place.

At the Tampa Bay Educational Leadership Collaborative (TELC) University of South Florida, two distinct programs have been developed—one for mentoring and one for coaching. Before either the coaching or mentoring programs began, staff-development training in mentoring or in coaching took place.

The mentoring program included new principals, in their first or second year of practice, who were mentored by retired school principals, superintendents, or administrators. Depending on which of the thirteen school districts participated in the program, either the principal selected the mentor—who might or not be from within the district—or the mentor was assigned to the principal. As issues came up for the new principals, they asked the mentors for advice. Some issues involved personnel: "I got this job, and it's one the vice principal wanted. How do I get her on board?" Or, "For the past ten years this teacher has had wonderful evaluations, yet I don't see his performance that way. How do I deal with that?" The mentor helped the new principal with the answers.

TELC describes its mentoring program as *a supportive relationship based on mutual trust and respect between an experienced professional and new principal.* It defines coaching as *an ongoing partnership that facilitates personal and professional support and development.* The focus of TELC's coaching program is to prepare a new level of executive leaders. They bring in coaches to work with district staff people at the supervisor level or above.

The staff person who wishes to be coached selects his or her coach—a retired administrator, superintendent, or other administrative-level person. The person being coached is being groomed to advance to a more executive level. The two spend time in a training session setting up expectations and developing their relationship. Coaching takes place weekly in ways they decide work best. Coaching can occur during frequent phone calls, instant messaging, e-mailing, live observation, or meeting for dinner or coffee—it can take whatever form, virtual or face-to-face, so long as there is weekly contact. The issues coached depend on the staff member's level of expertise and may include running faculty meetings, school improvement planning, increasing community involvement in the school, security, and safety.

The TELC program is just one example of many in the country where the purposes of a mentoring and coaching program are separately defined. The mentoring program tends to be fairly specific, whereas the coaching assumes certain equality and incorporates both personal and professional development on an ongoing basis.

At Hartford Union High School District in Wisconsin, there are also two distinct programs in place: collegial coaching and mentors for beginning teachers (referred to as "initial educators"). The mentoring program is mandatory for these initial educators in their first year only, unless it's decided that a teacher be mentored for another full year. Teacher's mentors are department chairs and focus on administrative matters and curriculum for teaching content.

The opportunity for collegial coaching exists within the mentoring program, both for the first year of teaching and then on an ongoing, voluntary basis. Teachers participating in the coaching program receive various incentives to continue with coaching, depending on how often they participate in a coaching observation session. The incentives include such things as tuition vouchers, compensatory days off, flextime, and attendance at national conventions—even free lunches!

The purpose of their coaching program is *to improve student achievement, professional success, and self-esteem.* Coaching can occur in class or through review of materials and videotapes. The program stresses that coaching is entirely nonevaluative and that any materials, comments, observations, or suggestions made to the person being coached "become the property of the coaches." Coaches assist teachers with classroom management, instructional strategies, motivation techniques, stress and time management, or any other strategy, technique, behavior, or attitude the coachee wants to improve.

The coachee-focused aspect of this program points up another key difference between coaching and mentoring. Where mentoring focuses on the knowledge of the mentor, coaching focuses on the one being coached. That person is asked what he or she wants to know, to accomplish, to improve—what does the coachee want the coach to observe?

Those being coached might also indicate how, when, and why they want feedback. The coachees reveal weaknesses or areas where they want to improve and ask for coaching on those issues only. The funnel is not open for coaches to pour in their own knowledge. The coach asks the questions; the coachee discovers the answers.

Another difference between coaching and mentoring is that in most school mentoring programs, mentors are assigned to teachers—they have no choice. In collegial coaching, the person being coached chooses who comes into his or her classroom, establishes the reason the coach is there, and determines what he or she wants the coach to observe. The choices are all in the coachee's court.

Mentoring and coaching each have their own purpose and strengths; each is important in the professional development of teachers. Relationship is paramount. Mentor and coach need to establish a level of trust with the one being coached or mentored, and vice versa. And communication is key.

The issue of trust is a big one. More and more schools are implementing mentor programs that pair beginning teachers with experienced colleagues. Principals realize that mentors are crucial to the survival, effectiveness, and satisfaction of beginning teachers and that they help to create a trusting environment quickly.

Yet the principal is also inevitably involved. New teachers find themselves in a position of having to both seek advice or get help from mentors while at the same time trying not to appear incompetent to their new "boss," the principal. The mentoring process is hampered as the new teacher is often excited and challenged about all he or she is learning, yet also cautious, fearful, or vulnerable. There are ways to set up a mentoring program that do not create this situation, as you will see.

FOUR MENTORING MODELS

When setting up a mentoring program, I recommend that the mentor, teacher, and their principal meet to establish norms for working together. They should identify how they will work with one other and how they will communicate. The following diagrams show four different models for how this can occur; there are undoubtedly others.

Model One: Two-Way Communication

In the Two-Way Communication Model, shown in figure 2.2, communication exists between the mentor and the teacher, and separate communi-

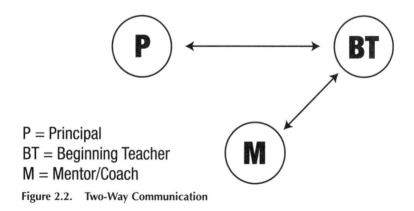

P = Principal
BT = Beginning Teacher
M = Mentor/Coach

Figure 2.2.   Two-Way Communication

cation takes place between the principal and the beginning teacher. By agreement, there will be no discussion between the mentor and the principal about the teacher.

The model assures the teacher that nothing he or she shares with the mentor will get back to the principal. Rather, the mentor gives the teacher opportunities to learn and correct any initial weaknesses or requests for assistance without the principal's knowing about them. Some beginning teachers, especially, feel more open to share weaknesses and to ask the mentor for help knowing that no information is shared with the principal, who ultimately will be doing the teacher's evaluation.

For example, a principal might tell a new teacher that she will be expected to work on a team of teachers to implement a student conduct program. The teacher may not fully understand the program yet may be hesitant to share her ignorance with the principal. Instead, she would turn to her mentor for insights and receive the information she needs without fear of repercussion or a negative evaluation.

The Two-Way Communication Model assumes an initial basic level of trust, yet it is a beginning step, the beginning teacher's movement through insecurity, and it addresses needs or desires the principal or the school system may have.

Model Two: The Silent Mentor

In the Silent Mentor Model, figure 2.3, the mentor *does* meet with the principal about the teacher. The principal may share concerns, desires, or questions about the teacher with the mentor, but the mentor *only listens* to

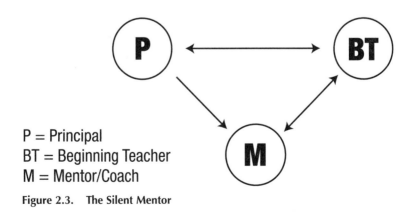

P = Principal
BT = Beginning Teacher
M = Mentor/Coach

Figure 2.3. The Silent Mentor

the principal's concerns and doesn't discuss the teacher at all. This procedure provides the same safeguards for the teacher as in the first model—freedom to be open with the mentor and yet security that no information passes to the principal. It also allows the mentor to understand issues or desires raised by the principal and to pass them on to the teacher in a productive fashion.

For example, if the principal expresses a concern that the teacher is not connecting learning activities to district assessments, the mentor would listen carefully and decide how best to work with the beginning teacher to accomplish the principal's goals. The principal would not pry into how the teacher was faring but would simply explain to the mentor what was to be improved—or, on a positive note, say what seemed encouraging about the teacher's ability to learn and work in the new situation.

This model allows for the mentor to earn the trust of the teacher. Trust often develops in the hiring process with the principal, yet teachers also need to form that level of trust with mentors for the program to succeed.

The teacher and principal continue to interact, as do the mentor and the teacher, but the mentor can decide in what way he or she can best help the teacher. Here again, the mentor serves as a buffer between teacher and principal, and lends a helping hand without the principal's direct involvement.

Model Three: Positive Reinforcement

As in Model Two, the Silent Mentor—the mentor in the third model, Positive Reinforcement, figure 2.4—has meetings with the principal regarding the teacher. In this model, however, there *is* discussion between mentor and principal about the teacher, but the mentor's comments focus *only on the teacher's positive growth*. Notice in figure 2.4 the line between the principal and mentor is shown as a dotted line. This indicates that only "good news" is shared with the principal. The principal can express areas where he or she thinks there should be improvement or where there is progress, but the mentor continues to reinforce only what is positive.

For example, the principal may comment to the mentor that the teacher needs to implement lesson plans in more depth. The mentor might reply, "John has just completed a great unit on the environment. You might want

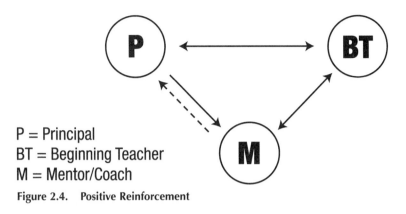

P = Principal
BT = Beginning Teacher
M = Mentor/Coach

Figure 2.4.   Positive Reinforcement

to take a look at it." The mentor reinforces the positive aspects of the teacher, helping the principal focus on what he or she is doing that seems to be working well.

Model Four: Full Communication

Model Four, Full Communication, figure 2.5, provides for the most open trust of the four models, and it is the one I believe principals, teachers, and mentors alike should choose as their model. It assumes that everyone is convinced that the teacher's success is the goal. If the principal sees a behavior or omission in teaching technique to be addressed, this model provides a forum to address it in a positive light. The principal serves as a supportive coach or mentor, working as a team with the teacher and mentor to ensure the teacher's success in the classroom.

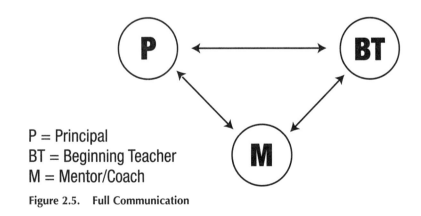

P = Principal
BT = Beginning Teacher
M = Mentor/Coach

Figure 2.5.   Full Communication

All three people are in an ongoing collaboration and open discussion about the teacher's progress. The teacher is empowered to provide new ideas, giving the principal-teacher-mentor relationship a strong base from which to operate. The process leads to improved morale, motivation, and performance by the teacher, enhancing student learning as a result.

An Example of Full Communication

A teacher in Hartford Union High School in Hartford, Wisconsin, has two girls in his sophomore English class whose behavior often creates disruption in the classroom. They talk, giggle, and leer at the teacher, making him feel intimidated.

In his meeting with the principal and his mentor, he shares his feelings without concern he will be chastised for not using better classroom-management skills. Rather, his colleagues collaborate with him and together develop strategies to deal with the situation. This gives him additional ideas he can use not only with the two sophomores but also with others. He discovers more options, boosting his confidence and motivation. As he employs these strategies in his classroom, the other students are relieved of the disruption, along with the teacher, the two girls are quieted, and more learning occurs.

It is this fourth model, Full Communication, that is closest to coaching as opposed to mentoring. There is a shared emphasis on the success of the person being coached, and that can occur whether the person is a new teacher, a long-term tenured educator, an assistant principal, or administrator.

The most significant similarity between coach and mentor in this model revolves around the nonevaluative nature of the relationship. Mentoring differs from the role of evaluator in that in most programs the mentor is not given evaluative capabilities. The principal in this model may offer suggestions or suggest ways the teacher might improve his or her approach, but no evaluation takes place. The fourth model differs from coaching in that the coachees do not pick their own mentors.

In short, no one is being judged here. Mentor, principal, and coach are supporting the teacher, whether to learn the ropes of a new school or situation or to improve and enhance his or her professional development on an ongoing basis.

EVALUATION

An evaluator uses a skill set entirely different from those of either mentor or coach. Criteria on which one person evaluates another are controlled and come from outside the relationship between teacher and principal. Evaluators work for "the system," such as a school district or state. Their task is to protect the system from incompetence. Minimum competencies are defined by the system, and the evaluator checks that a teacher meets them. An evaluator may be the principal or an administrator—either of whom may also want to consider themselves coaches. This is where a level of trust with the teacher can break down.

"I" Messages: Evaluation and Assessment

I often do an "I" message activity when I'm training coaches to see the differences between the feeling of being *evaluated* and that of having one's skills *assessed*. I ask participants to pair up and decide who will be Partner A and who will be Partner B. Partner A notices something about Partner B's appearance. It could be clothing, eyeglasses, height, color of hair, or shape of nose.

A then tells B what he or she noticed by beginning a sentence with the word "you." "You look great in red." "Your eyeglasses are broken." "You're sure tall!"

They do this a few times each, and then I ask them how it felt. I hear comments such as "self-conscious," "like a guinea pig," "embarrassed," "defensive." Because the sentence begins with a "you," it automatically implies judgment and evaluation. They hear the other person's opinion of who they are or how they appear. Whether or not it matches their own, it creates a self-consciousness that can be uncomfortable or even insulting.

They do the exercise again. This time Partner A notices something about B's appearance. Then he or she shares what was noticed by beginning the sentence with "I." "I like you in red." "I always wanted to be tall like you. How tall are you?" (They can also ask questions.)

When prompted for how each partner felt, the responses are usually "good," "important," "complimented," "cared for," "noticed." When I ask them why, they say it is because the other person took responsibility for what they noticed and their opinion about it. It didn't come across as judgmental, and therefore they didn't feel self-conscious or uncomfortable—it was just the other person's opinion.

The point is that evaluation uses an indirect "you" message. It puts people on the defensive, off guard, ill at ease, even when they receive positive or complimentary evaluations. An evaluation judges a person based on criteria developed from someone else's set of beliefs, opinions, or ideas about the correct way of teaching.

In a coaching model, the process leans more toward assessment. When a coach assesses someone, personal thoughts and feelings surface. It is not the cold objectiveness of evaluation. A coach notices certain behaviors about the coachee's teaching—both those behaviors on which the teacher asked the coach to focus as well as others that the coach noticed on his or her own. The coach then asks the teacher if he or she can share personal observations. The coachee has the option to say yes or no.

If the coach gives his or her personal feedback, it is given as an implied or direct "I" message: "I saw—felt, heard—this when you implemented that strategy or reflected on your behavior." Hearing an "I" message, coachees can respond more openly and freely. They are not burdened by the coach's judgment or evaluation. What the coach noticed or felt is simply what was noticed; it's not necessarily the right or wrong way of doing things.

Principals often believe they are in a coaching role, helping a teacher improve performance. In my experience, principals feel they are evaluating 60 percent of the time and coaching 40 percent. Teachers, however, feel it's more like 95 percent evaluation to 5 percent coaching. It's all in perception. The teacher's perception is that the principal is evaluating, not coaching, and the principal thinks the opposite. They're both telling the truth in terms of their *perceptions*. I have found when I introduce a coaching program to a school district that includes principals and administrators as participants that the perception of evaluation quickly wanes as they learn the value, behaviors, and skills of true coaching.

To make the principal's role clear, you can establish the following criterion. If a principal is invited into a teacher's classroom room, it's coaching. If the principal comes without invitation, it's evaluation or supervision.

The figure 2.1 continuum, on page 24, shows on a spectrum where the differences in the roles of evaluator, supervisor, mentor, and coach fall.

This model requires that trust weave throughout the roles. Teachers want their evaluations to be fair, and many researchers feel there should even be inter-rater agreement when evaluating—that is, the teacher would receive the same evaluation regardless of who came to evaluate, because the criteria would be standard. Most schools lack such a standard, however, so when the principal or outside evaluator changes, all scores change too.

Typically, an evaluation is based on minimum competencies, and educators are graded on whether they meet those competencies. This practice undermines the trust level and the professionalism of teachers—they don't like to get good grades for doing the minimum. It completely goes against the concept of moving from good to great teaching. Once an evaluation is completed, the person evaluating washes his or her hands of the issue. It's the score sheet, not them, that dictates the teacher's future performance. The evaluator does not make suggestions for improvement; coaches do. They are separated from the evaluation instrument.

SUPERVISION

Stranded in the middle of this continuum is the supervisor. While this may often be the principal, there are several people in a school who might have the title of "supervisor." Supervisors are responsible for evaluation based on a set of criteria, such as state guidelines, school board policies, union contracts, etc. They are also responsible for satisfying the desires, motivations, and goals of the individuals of their teaching staff—teacher growth. This requires them to behave more like coaches. In short, where an evaluator might just evaluate and a coach just coach, a supervisor may do both, trying to cover both ends of the spectrum.

Given differences in purpose, philosophy, skill, and attitude, it is possible to do both, but difficult. The problem is that the teacher never knows the supervisor's role, so the trust level is low. The supervisor may exhibit convincing behaviors to let the teacher know he or she has the teacher's best interest at heart. The supervisor may refer to it as "our" evaluation session, when in fact it is the teacher's evaluation. But how does the teacher perceive it?

Often supervisors or principals play all the roles on the continuum. A principal or an administrator comes in to do an evaluation, supervise, mentor, and coach. Human nature being what it is, however, when teachers have weaknesses—and everyone knows their weaknesses—they certainly never want to show it during evaluation sessions. On the other hand, when someone comes in to coach, teachers may be more willing to focus on their weaknesses so they can get properly coached.

Because teachers become confused about how to behave with the person who walks into their room unless they know the person's role in advance, I often suggest that the principal or supervisor literally wear different colored hats depending on the role they're playing—evaluator, supervisor, mentor, or coach. When the teacher sees the hat color, he or she knows which "role" just walked into the room.

Another idea is for the principal or supervisor to copy the continuum on page 24, laminate it, and carry it around, pointing out to the teacher with a pen mark where he or she is on the continuum at that moment.

Clarity in roles should be replicated by teachers as they work with students. They should change "hats" whenever they are changing roles so that students know who they are dealing with and what they can expect. The teacher as a coach makes suggestions for improvements; the teacher as an evaluator grades tests.

SUMMARY

The intent of all roles associated with education is to teach students. In the process of teaching, the teacher needs constantly to change gears, improve, learn, change, grow, and adjust. Mentors help teachers learn the ropes and untie difficult knots along the way. Principals or supervisors, in their roles, ensure that teachers are up to standards—that they are in fact performing well and, if not, working on ways to improve. Coaches work on the side of teachers to help them be and do all they are capable of, by addressing specific issues teachers need and want to work on.

All roles are interchangeable as long as everyone knows who's on first—the role each is playing and why. That knowledge builds trust and paves the way for teachers to improve their skills in a safe environment. Ultimately, the student benefits the most.

In chapter 3, we'll take a look at exactly what coaching is—how it plays out in terms of improving skill, knowledge, and behavior. Also, we'll look again at the issues of trust and quality, and at how both principal and coach can interchange roles to support the one being coached or evaluated.

3

Okay, What *Is* Coaching?

We've looked at the various roles in coaching, but what exactly is this thing called "coaching"? Coaching creates an opportunity for two individuals to enter into an ongoing dialogue and relationship, the focus of which is to improve skills, techniques, and behaviors that lead to professional and personal success.

Coaching entails a profound and dynamic practice applied in a variety of ways for a lot of good reasons. It is used in sports, personal relationships, by business entrepreneurs, in marriages, and wherever support, feedback, and a mutual commitment to change and growth are desired. This book focuses on coaching and teaching where a coach supports a teacher in improving his or her skills in order to improve teaching and student learning. Coaching, then, becomes integrally tied to an educator's professionalism and students' achievements.

Coaching in the private sector consists of a professional relationship in which the coach is paid for his or her services. In teaching, coaching focuses on improving professionalism, and the coach provides this service as part of a coaching or mentoring program established by the school or district or through a peer relationship with a fellow teacher.

While certainly friendship might occur in the process, coaching is not about making friends. A friend might support another without necessarily working toward improving that person's behavior. A coach, on the other hand, focuses on allowing the coachee to commit to positive change and then supports that person in the effort to accomplish that change. Coaching for educators has a specific focus—improving teaching. Coaching is not just limited to two people supporting one another in their profession. As we shall see later in this book, when carried out with quality, coaching follows a well-defined process and utilizes finely tuned verbal skills and questioning techniques to achieve the desired outcome.

Supporting someone willing to make changes, guiding them toward stretching and improving, giving them useful feedback, and otherwise jumping into their life requires a high level of trust on the part of both parties. This type of coaching provides a type of professional staff development training that uncovers ways to improve specific techniques or behaviors through observation and feedback. The coaching process is meant to give a coachee sufficient skill and practice so that transfer occurs and skills and techniques become naturally ingrained.

Coaching also gives those being coached an opportunity for conversation with other like-minded professionals. It provides a forum to develop collegial relationships that enhance self-esteem and professionalism. This, in turn, improves teaching, which improves student learning.

In *Motivating Students and Teachers in an Era of Standards*, Richard Sagor (2003) makes the following observation concerning what motivates educators:

> The classroom teacher's need for belonging is often overlooked in schools. . . . School administrators occasionally and incorrectly assume that because teachers are granted considerable autonomy within the walls of their classrooms, they don't have a professional need for collegiality and community.
>
> In environments where workers have come to feel like members of high-performing teams and regularly get to enjoy the camaraderie of their coworkers, higher levels of performance are invariably produced (Senge 1990; Senge 1999). It is imperative that teaching be restructured into a more collaborative and collegial endeavor. (p. 9)

Voilà coaching.

INSTANCE OF ONE

Research shows learning occurs best when there is a relationship involved. Think about a time, a specific occasion that occurred in your life when someone taught you something quickly—in one try or in one instance.

Choose a task, a skill, or an action that you were taught one time and that you never forgot. You were immediately successful, and you have known how to do it or use it from that time forward. Examples might be tying your shoes, riding a bike, washing dishes, or later in life, understanding an equation, setting up a computer, using pause time effectively in the classroom.

In these instances, there is typically someone present—someone with whom you have a relationship. Whatever was taught was taught in a safe environment. The consequences of what you were learning were real to you, and you may have experienced an emotion. In short, the experience was probably a positive one with the person teaching you basking in your success right along with you. That is the true nature of learning and the true nature of coaching. *The coach succeeds when you succeed.*

GORDON'S LADDER

Three outcomes of a coaching process include the opportunity for celebration and personal recognition; the opportunity for developing a wider array of options; and the opportunity to participate in "conscious practice." Let's use the model in figure 3.1, developed by William Gordon to show how these coaching opportunities occur.

Gordon's model is called a Skill Development Ladder. In it he identifies the process one goes through when beginning a task not previously undertaken. For our example, let's use the basic teaching technique called "pause time." The teacher takes a three-to-five-second pause after asking a question, after calling a student by name, and again after a student has answered a question. Likewise, pause time can be used when a teacher puts forth a new idea or concept.

Pausing when asking a question benefits teacher and student alike, as we shall see later. When putting forth a new idea, it is often beneficial to pause and allow the thought to linger in the air a little before the students absorb it. In our fast-paced world, we often move from thought to thought quickly. Pause time allows thinking and learning to take place.

Pausing at first may seem awkward, contrived. It's hard enough for a teacher to keep track of the questions as students are answering them, how much time remains—even the students' names—much less mentally counting out three or five seconds!

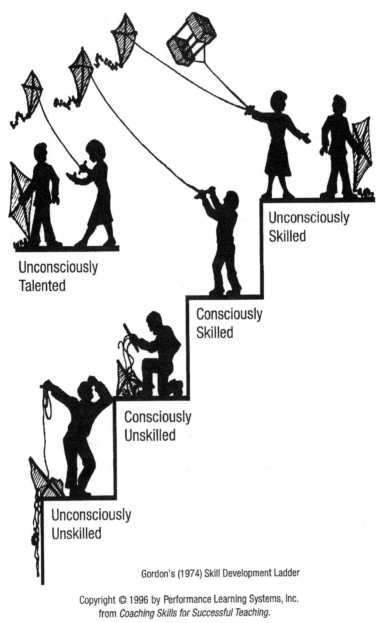

Unconsciously
Talented

Unconsciously
Skilled

Consciously
Skilled

Consciously
Unskilled

Unconsciously
Unskilled

Gordon's (1974) Skill Development Ladder

Copyright © 1996 by Performance Learning Systems, Inc.
from *Coaching Skills for Successful Teaching*.

Figure 3.1.   Gordon's Skill Development Ladder

Enter Gordon's Ladder. On the lower rung you see a teacher—let's call her Becky. Becky has never heard of pause time, never used it, and never thought about it. This teacher is Unconsciously Unskilled in that technique. She hasn't a clue.

On the next rung, Becky now knows that pause time is a valuable tool that should be used in her classroom. She has learned that at least three seconds of pause should occur after a question is posed and before the teacher calls on a student by name. After calling the student's name, there should be another three-second pause. Jumping in too fast or moving to the next person too quickly undermines a student's self-esteem. Time is needed for the student to form a thought and respond without teacher interference.

Pausing after a question is posed also allows the teacher time to review the question for its appropriateness and understandability, determine whom to call on, and assess who might likely know the right answer. Pausing three seconds after calling the student's name gives the teacher time to decide what would constitute a complete answer.

Once the student answers the question, the teacher should pause five seconds. This gives the student time to elaborate, ask questions, make a student-to-student exchange, and build confidence in the process. Less vocal students, when given that breathing space, can feel comfortable contributing as well. Pausing helps learning, and that's what Becky wants to do.

So, while she is aware of its value and knows something about the technique, she isn't skilled in its use. In fact, she may have been using it before, but now that she is *conscious* of the technique, it suddenly feels uncomfortable, unnatural. She is Consciously Unskilled, and is on the second rung of Gordon's Ladder.

In Becky's case, at the Consciously Unskilled level, she posed a question for the class, and then she paused, her arm in midair and her body very still, as if suddenly frozen. She counted in her head and looked a little silly, and yet she really did know what to do—she may have done it hundreds of times in the past. She may be conscious of what she's doing, but the new knowledge about the skill and her actual behavior has not meshed—it's not yet internalized or natural. Thus, she comes across as awkward. This happens to many of us when learning a new sport or task that requires the combination of knowledge and performance. We know the *what* of it but not the *how*. It's easy to become frustrated, and because we're conscious of our lack of skill, even embarrassed.

Enter Becky's coach. This is where the coach provides feedback, support, celebration, and serves as Becky's "cheerleader," helping her practice in a safe environment without concern about how she looks the first few times out. The coach can make the coachee feel comfortable with his or her discomfort, because the mutual goal continues to be the improvement of teaching. If one goes through a little discomfort to get there, well, so be it.

When I first began teaching, I asked my coach for feedback on my presentation skills and ability to engage students. She pointed out that I tended to keep my hands in my pockets when I was talking. Worse, I jingled my keys and pocket change around, creating a distraction that lessened student engagement.

To remedy this, we agreed that she would observe me teaching and that whenever I put my hands in my pockets, she would make a gesture of putting her finger on her forehead. That would signal to me to take my hands out of my pocket.

I began the lesson, and after a while, sure enough, my hands were in my pockets. I saw her signal, and boom! Out came the hands, flying up into the air. That seemed a safe place, so I continued talking and moving about the room with hands held wide and high. Muttered comments from students indicated perhaps I had had too much caffeine that morning!

This stilted behavior is typical of anyone who becomes conscious of a new skill. We experience what is called a "Learning Dip," shown on page 45, figure 3.2.

The Learning Dip

Discomfort using the new skill causes confusion, and learning suffers a little at first. With continued observation, support, celebration, and feedback from a coach, the skill level climbs to a higher level, and more options become available to the teacher.

Once a coachee has practiced a skill and has it internalized, he or she moves up to the Consciously Skilled rung on Gordon's Ladder. The coach's observation and feedback is also crucial on this rung of the ladder. The skill can be accomplished so long as the person is thinking about

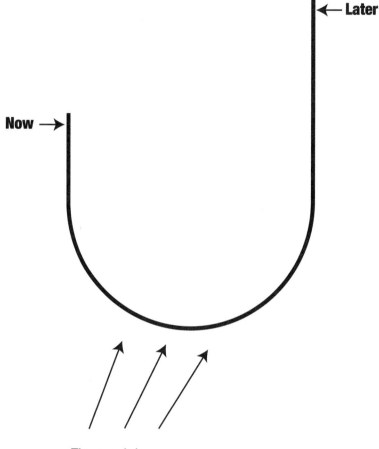

The coach is a
cheerleader during
this difficult time.

Figure 3.2. The Learning Dip

it, aware of it, practicing it in his or her head. In our example, Becky may pose a question, think about pausing three seconds, and then call on the student. She knows the *what* and the *how*, so long as she *consciously* thinks about it. This works, yet the behavior does not appear as smooth and natural—nor as easy—as it is on the next rung of the ladder, Unconsciously Skilled.

On the Unconsciously Skilled rung, the skill is ingrained. It is used naturally and well. No longer does Becky have to think about it, count seconds, or otherwise be concerned that she is not providing enough pause time. She has been observed doing it, she has practiced it, she has received feedback from her coach (and also, ideally, from a videotape). She has practiced so often that it is ingrained in her. She does it without thought. This rung is where teachers want to be—skilled but unconscious of the skill or behavior—so that it is a natural part of their performance and does not get in the way of their teaching or student learning. I've often said teachers do their best work when they're unconscious!

I will grant that our example of pause time is basic, chosen to underscore the process in the Skill Development Ladder. Yet the same process applies for more complex teaching skills and techniques, such as creating and delivering a math lesson that reaches all learning styles, incorporating content learning into a high school field trip, using the right voice intonation to ensure better classroom management, and, for administrators, facilitating a meeting, interviewing a potential employee, or prioritizing action plans.

The Hartford Union High School coaching program in Hartford, Wisconsin, provides another example. Here a teacher wanted to facilitate presentations given by students. She wanted specific feedback on her *facilitation* skills and her ability to keep students engaged. While she had teaching skills down pat, her skills at facilitating—moving the discussion along without contributing much herself—tended to be awkward. She was at the Consciously Unskilled Level. Her coach observed her facilitating, and she accomplished the skill, yet her body language indicated she was "biting her tongue."

In another example, a technical education teacher at Hartford asked his students to create race cars out of blocks of wood. They had to first design a car on the computer using specifications, and then create cars using saws and other machinery. Later students would compete in a race with their cars. The teacher wanted to ensure he was focusing on *all* students in the room, despite their variety of tasks. This was a new project, and he wanted to make sure he was as "there" for them as he was in a single-focus lesson plan. His coach confirmed that he was.

You will notice that off to the side of Gordon's Skill Development Ladder I have added another "rung" of my own—perhaps it's the place where one can put the can of paint on a real ladder. This category is called Unconsciously Talented. Here the person exhibiting the skill or behavior does so without the benefit of any specific process of skill development or coaching. This person is naturally talented; he or she can perform moves or work through teaching strategies seemingly effortlessly. Unconsciously Talented educators do not know either the *what* or the *how* of their actions; they simply perform them.

Are these the "great teachers" we spoke of in chapter 1? Certainly they are good teachers, yet they lack an ability inherent in the Unconsciously Skilled teacher—they are unable to articulate what they do. They cannot mentor others very well due to this lack of self-knowledge; more importantly, they are unaware of the skills they do know, so they cannot be coached to improve them.

In a coaching relationship, coachees must ask to be coached on specific skills or behavioral developments in order to improve their teaching. The Unconsciously Talented person wouldn't know what to ask for. So, in my book, great teachers are Unconsciously Skilled teachers. Certainly, Unconsciously Talented teachers are good, but the difference lies in their understanding of their need to grow, change, improve, and enhance their professional teaching abilities.

TRUST

Coaches are judged by the performance of those they coach, whether teachers, administrators, staff people, or other professionals. In education, the success of the coach becomes tied to the success of the coachee, much as the success of a basketball coach is determined by the success of the players. A coach is a performance-based supporter.

Paramount in any coaching relationship is trust. Trust means saying what you're going to do and then doing it. When looking at the various roles of evaluating, supervising, coaching, and mentoring, we saw how crucial the element of trust is to the process. Someone who coaches you can never come across as an evaluator, judge, or supervisor, or they damage the coaching relationship. Trust serves as the foundation of the relationship between coach and coachee.

This does not mean that a principal cannot be assigned the role of coach. In many cases, they are. Administrators can give up their supervisory role and serve as mentor or coach if they say that is what they are going to do and then do it. The principal must take care to play the part of the coach when coaching and then clearly change to the role of supervisor when supervising. It's perfectly all right to switch back and forth. Here's the difference.

When principals (administrators, supervisors, or evaluators) evaluate, they are really looking for weaknesses or challenges a teacher has that need attention and improvement. Either the principal identifies the weakness or challenge, or the teacher comes forth and shares it. This differs from coaching, where the coachee asks to be coached on a specific skill or behavior.

The principal and teacher can opt to switch into a coaching relationship and work on the weakness or challenge, but that work then does not become a part of an official evaluation. It could be said that once a teacher is professional enough to express to the principal what he or she wants to work on, the principal can assume the teacher is competent enough to teach. Teachers with that much reflection, self-knowledge, and commitment to improve teaching don't need evaluation or supervision and can benefit from coaching.

When the principal provides coaching, he or she works with the teacher, not for "the system." If the principal is effective as a coach, he or she should then be able to evaluate the teacher later and see an improvement. The weakness or challenge should have been overcome. Once again, the improvement of the coachee reflects the success of the coach. It's to the principal's advantage to coach and create improvement. If, however, principals change behaviors in midstream—switches from coach to evaluator without saying what they intend to do—then all bets are off. Trust is broken, and the coaching relationship will be damaged and, very likely, ineffective thereafter.

QUALITY AND COMPLIANCE

Why do we make such a fuss over the distinction between evaluating and coaching? Research on how the brain operates in its highest level of productivity suggests that when people are empowered, they take ownership of their own learning and effectiveness.

The third edition of Susan Kovalik's seminal book *ITI: The Model, Integrated Thematic Instruction* (1997) explores eight elements that need to be present in order for the human brain to learn and operate at its best:

- Absence of threat
- Meaningful content
- Choices
- Adequate time
- Enriched environment
- Collaboration
- Immediate feedback
- Mastery

All eight are present in a coaching environment. In an evaluation, most of them may not be. The teacher usually receives little choice about the time, place, or specifics on which he or she will be evaluated. A time constraint usually exists, as the principal walks into the room unexpectedly, and the teacher hastens to get to the "good" part of the lesson or presentation. The teacher may become uncomfortable, as he or she is taken off guard, and may feel vulnerable, if not actually threatened. Often little collaboration or immediate feedback takes place, and the content may be meaningful only to the evaluator or the system. Since the teachers have no say in what is being evaluated, the evaluation lacks meaning for them.

In a coaching relationship, two people work together in a *collaborative*, trusting, and therefore, *enriched environment*. Initially they meet in an environment where trust develops and an *absence of threat* exists. This place might be the teacher's classroom, where he or she feels safe. *Collaboration* occurs as the coach and teacher work together on what the *teacher chooses* to improve. Since it's something the teacher really wants to know or be able to do, it holds *meaning* for the teacher. *Adequate time* exists to practice, receive *immediate feedback*, and thus create an opportunity for *mastery*.

In short, in a coaching environment, the coachee is fully engaged. The brain operates at its optimum in terms of learning about oneself and performing most productively.

UNIVERSAL MOTIVATION

In coaching, there also exists a need for motivation. In the third edition of *The Quality School: Managing Students Without Coercion* (1998), William Glasser, M.D., identifies five universals that motivate people:

- Survival
- Belonging
- Power
- Freedom
- Fun

Let's look at Glasser's motivators in terms of teaching and coaching.

Survival

Survival motivates people when they approach something new, make a change, take on a new task, or move to a new location or job. The motivating factor is to *survive*: to learn the ropes, do the right thing, find one's way, avoid getting lost. A beginning teacher is in a state of survival, and so too is a teacher new to a school, or a newly hired principal, or someone who just retired. All need to take on new "worlds" of people, tasks, rules, and events. The need to survive in their new situations motivates their behavior.

Belonging

The need to be accepted by others motivates—to be included, to receive approval, and to be liked. Once people realize they are going to survive in their new surroundings or job, they become motivated to join others. They may sign up for a committee or volunteer for a task after school. They want belonging and the approval that brings, so they will be motivated to put their best foot forward when someone is evaluating or observing them.

Power

Things start to look up for the new teacher. After surviving an initial learning curve and having acceptance of others, people begin to experience a sense of power. They know how to do what they need to do! They can even excel! This gives them a sense of personal power, and it also puts them in a position where others begin showing more respect or asking for advice. Power here means competence—the motivation to be competent at what one does so as to sense the feeling of power.

Freedom

Now things are cooking! The survival period is over, people seem to be accepted by others, they have a sense of competence and power. Now what? Now they are motivated by flexibility—the freedom they can enjoy stemming from their competence, belonging, and ability to survive. They have freedom to choose: choose lesson plans, choose themes for the school year, and choose to collaborate with other teachers. A sense of freedom inspires people. They take real ownership of their work, and it leads to creativity and quality.

Fun

Now they're having fun. When the motivation is fun, people jump out of bed to come to work. They already enjoy a sense of power and freedom (they've long since surpassed survival and belonging), and now they just want to enjoy what they do. They use all their resources—intelligence, social skills, creativity, research, camaraderie, and knowledge—to make every day enjoyable. Days go by quickly and well. Students respond with enthusiasm, and their motivation spreads to others. They develop quality work and produce it in others.

In my experience, when heavy-handed bosses or systems impose strict standards on others, people are typically motivated only by survival and belonging. They want to meet the criteria (survival), and they want their work to be accepted (belonging). In short, they comply with what is being asked of them. That's about all.

When there is collaboration, when coaching is taking place, when people are allowed to take ownership of their own learning and their own professional improvement, they are motivated by power, freedom, and fun. A sense of belonging shores up coaching, and the coaching process in and of itself gives way to increasing feelings of competence and power. Tremendous freedom results where one can explore behaviors and techniques that could be enhanced or learned. Also, it's fun to improve; it's really fun to have a coach—your own personal cheerleader—willing to give you feedback and support. When that occurs, walls come down and people are willing and able not only to comply with what is needed but to far exceed it and produce quality work.

Evaluations are necessary to track progress and comply with various mandates and even federal laws. To the extent that the environment and the empowerment of those being evaluated are enhanced by collaborative and collegial coaching, quality, and overall productivity, the enjoyment of teaching increases. Because of how the brain comes to life when elements such as absence of threat, choices, collaboration, and immediate feedback are available, a teacher can both comply with what is required of him or her, and enjoy the power, freedom, and fun in the process. Here's where teachers and students alike can experience a wow day; celebrations are in order, and both morale and student learning are sky high.

Coaching requires relationship. It requires trust. Coaching is brain based—it allows teachers to operate in ways that allow them to be more productive, creative, and empowered. Coaching becomes essential supporting teachers learning new tasks or new skills, moving them from the awkward Consciously Unskilled level of performance to one where the skill comes naturally, without thought or concern. Coaching requires the motivation of survival, belonging, power, freedom, and fun.

FIERCE CONVERSATIONS

Coaching really entails conversation. Susan Scott, a coach of many years to CEOs from some of the largest international corporations, encapsulates her ideas about coaching in her book *Fierce Conversations* (2002). By "fierce," Scott does not mean threatening or cruel. Rather she takes the original meaning of "fierce" and synonyms from *Roget's Thesaurus*: "robust, intense, strong, powerful, passionate, eager, unbridled, uncurbed, untamed." Wow! Imagine the possibilities of that!

When was the last time you had an "untamed" or "robust" conversation? How often have you had conversations with coworkers or family members that were bland, meaningless, or significantly less than "fierce"? In fact, evaluations are often bland and meaningless to the person being evaluated. Many conversations are depleted of meaning and lacking authenticity. They just fill a void. Scott's contention is the conversation *is* the relationship. The level of the conversation between people—its intensity, power, unbridled nature—reflects the level of the relationship.

In coaching, the conversation between the coach and the coachee forms the key to the relationship. Communication creates the trust—saying what you will do and then doing it. It uncovers the coachee's agenda, vision, and beliefs. It helps explore options and strategies, tactics, and the focus of the teaching, along with the personal and professional development of the individual.

SUMMARY

In many ways, coaching involves a unique relationship. It consists of a supportive and nurturing dialogue between two people, yet it also asks one to stretch, grow, and improve. This may or may not be a comfortable task, yet the coach provides the tools, techniques, and guidance to make it possible.

Coaching becomes particularly useful when a teacher learns a new skill or behavior. As we saw in Gordon's Skill Development Ladder, discomfort, awkwardness, and even a little intimidation can occur at certain rungs on the ladder. As a teacher progresses, the coach cheers the coachee on. Coaching increases the coachee's ability to persevere and succeed as he or she climbs up the rungs of the ladder to utilize skilled teaching strategies.

Substantial research shows how the brain lights up when learning and empowerment occur. Coaching allows a coachee to achieve quality, as opposed to simple compliance. The coaching relationship utilizes many of the elements of brain-compatible learning and working techniques, allowing people being coached to excel at their own pace and within a safe environment of learning.

Coaching also opens up the possibilities for teachers to work together as a team to help individual students. It paves the way for a new kind of school where students belong to the whole school—or at least to a focus group of teachers who share in the success of each student. While many schools may give lip service to this kind of teaching atmosphere, coaching can ensure that it occurs.

Coaching is a means to an end. The end result is an improved teacher and thus improved teaching. It is a professional relationship that causes positive actions to occur.

In chapter 4, we'll explore ways in which your conversation—your communication—with your coach and with others can move from bland to fierce, gaining momentum and meaning at each step of the way.

4

The Skills of Coaching

The coaching process includes a series of conversations between the coach and coachee. Initially, the conversation takes place in what we call a "preobservation conference." After the person being coached has been observed in a classroom, doing a specific lesson plan, conducting a meeting, reflecting on his or her growth and improvement, or other situations where the coachee wants feedback, it is followed by a "postobservation" conference. We explore this process later on in the book.

The purpose of the initial conversation—the preobservation conference—determines what the coachee wants the coach to observe, what specific feedback he or she seeks, or what behaviors or techniques the coachee wants to improve or enhance. If this is to be done in a way that serves both the coach and the coachee, certain coaching skills must be in place. This ensures that the process is effective, and it also creates the essential ingredient of trust between the coach and the person being coached.

AGENDA SKILLS FOR COACHING

People behave in certain ways for their own reasons—their agenda. Likewise, individuals will change their behavior for their own reasons. When one clearly understands what goes on in a person's mind, then a communication strategy can be used that will be congruent with his or her self-interest.

Agenda Skills for Coaching described below help coaches discover their coachee's agenda as well as provide techniques to ensure a trusting relationship. While you may recognize and even use some of these skills, I have adapted them to a coaching relationship because, as we shall see later, beyond uncovering a person's agenda, the coachee must also reveal his or her vision, mission, or beliefs behind his or her strategies and behavior.

Open-Ended and Closed-Ended Questions

The first two agenda skills are open- and closed-ended questions. These questioning skills help you find the coachee's agenda—what he or she thinks, intends; what is wanted or needed; and his or her reasons for behaving in certain ways.

When asked an open-ended question, the person being asked has the opportunity to express what's on his or her mind, to explain what he or she considers important. These questions allow a wide range of responses and provide the opportunity for sharing thoughts, feelings, or ideas freely. They are useful in learning the story behind the facts, the reasoning, the assumptions, or the background of a situation or piece of information.

Closed-ended questions, on the other hand, limit the length of a person's response to a few words. They elicit yes/no or short responses. Think of the TV cop shows where people ask for "just the facts." Closed-ended questions are useful in gathering data. They are helpful when a precise piece of information is required. They focus directly on a specific point and limit the opportunity for the person to elaborate.

Asking closed-ended questions is efficient. Yet ultimately, the open-ended question may actually be even more efficient, because while the response may be longer, it allows the coachee to explain the reasoning and assumptions leading up to a response. This paves the way for more open, "fierce" conversation between the coach and the coachee.

A closed-ended question controls the direction of communication. The person asking can control where the conversation goes. In the open-ended question, the answer controls the direction—the person is given the leeway to respond fully and leads the direction of the conversation.

The continuum in figure 4.1 shows how the environment—the circumstances leading to the purpose of your questioning—influences whether a

The Environment Influences When the Question Is Open and When It Is Closed.

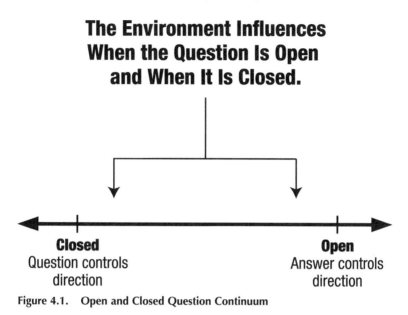

Closed
Question controls
direction

Open
Answer controls
direction

Figure 4.1.   Open and Closed Question Continuum

question is "closed" (where the question controls the direction) or "open" (where the answer controls the direction).

Examples of closed-ended questions a coach may ask a coachee follow:

- "At what point did you notice that most of your students were with you?" (The answer to this closed-ended question would be a specific time or incident; a short response, e.g., "Right after we hung the posters".)
- "What emotions did you feel when Olivia made that smart remark?" ("Angry, frustrated"—a short, specific response.)
- "Would you like to rehearse alternative responses?" ("Yes." "No." "Not now." "Maybe.")
- "Did you know that gesturing with your open hand is perceived as more friendly than pointing?" ("You don't say!" etc.)
- "Did you know that you have excellent eye contact with all students in the room?" ("Thank you.")
- "Where can I sit that would make you feel most comfortable?" ("In the back." "By the window." "On the left side of the room." etc.)
- "Did you notice that when you moved close to Toni's desk, she got back to work?" ("Yes!")

- "At what point in your lesson did you feel the most successful?" "Why?" (Closed-ended question followed by an open-ended question.)
- "What strategies in your lesson would you like to improve?" "Why?" (Closed-ended question followed by an open-ended question.)
- "In what areas do you want to be coached?" ("Engaging students." "Rotating my teaching style." "Going over homework assignments." "My new math lesson." "Eye contact." "Gestures and body language." Etc.)

As mentioned earlier, open-ended questions allow maximum latitude for the other person to share, elaborate, and express. As you read through open-ended questions below, imagine how you might answer them, noting how they would lead to revealing a lot about your background, beliefs, and feelings.

- "What are your strengths as a teacher?"
- "How would you know if your lesson was successful?"
- "What have you considered as areas of growth for the year?"
- "How do you think coaching will benefit your teaching?"
- "If there were no curriculum, what would you be teaching?" "Why?"
- "How would you describe a 'good' lesson?" "A 'great' lesson?"
- "If you were a student, what kind of teacher would you like to have?"
- "How could I be the most help to you?"
- "What do you feel contributed to your success today?"
- "Imagine it is the end of the school year. What would you want to say about the year?"
- "If you could change anything, what would you change in education?"

You may have noticed most open-ended questions begin with "what" or "how." They may also begin with "why," although a word of caution is necessary here. Questions such as "Why did you do that?" and "How could you have handled him differently?" can work against you, because they often lead to a defensive response rather than obtain information. This can occur even if the question is delivered with neutral or positive intonation. "What" and "how" questions may be linked in people's brains with the assumption they have done something wrong, that they're in trouble, especially if asked by someone they consider an authority figure. As a coach, you want to be a collaborator, not an authority figure, to continue to develop trust and open communication. Ask "why" questions about positive issues to break the connection that you are implying something is "wrong."

Here's an example of asking a "why" questions with a positive outcome:

> Coach: "Why did you open with the song from World War II?"
> Teacher: "I thought it would be unexpected and capture the student's attention."
> Coach: "It looked to me as if it did just that. Several students laughed and were singing along. That's very brain compatible: music, fun, and nonthreatening."

Repeating a positive pattern assures the coachee that the "why" questions are meant to uncover his or her thinking, not point to a problem in delivery. Also, the attitude and positive body language of the coach adds to a successful outcome of the conversation.

While asking closed-ended and open-ended questions may seem fairly straightforward, people tend to pose only closed-ended questions. As in any skill, practice is necessary to internalize asking these two types of questions. Research shows that twenty to thirty trials of a new skill or procedure are necessary to achieve comfort and control (Joyce, Wolf, & Calhoun 1993).

Practice

See if you can change the following closed-ended questions into open-ended questions. Phrase them in your mind or jot them down here. Suggested examples of how these can be changed are found on page 78 at the end of this chapter:

- "Do you think your lesson will turn out well?"
- "Did you think the students were interested?"
- "Give me another reason."
- "What are you going to try now?"
- "What part would you change?"
- "When does it end?"

By learning to ask good questions and make statements appropriate to a coaching situation, you will learn to formulate dialogue that stimulates thinking, reveals a person's agenda, and generates more understanding. More understanding generates more trust. Make a point to use open-ended questions throughout your day. Begin the sentence with "what" or "how" or a gentle "why." Remember you want a broad-based response, so the question should be phrased in such a way that the other person can be expressive; share the background, feelings, and intent—to tell, as radio commentator Paul Harvey says, "the *rest* of the story."

Yes, it takes longer to listen to the responses to open-ended questions. Yet in the long run, you will have gained valuable knowledge about the coachee and your next encounter can be more in-depth. You can start where you left off. A certain amount of trust will have been built—an openness that allows you to "cut to the chase" a lot sooner.

Another tip: Word your questions so the answer is neither right nor wrong. "What did you notice?" "What do you want to have happen?" The coach accepts all answers; there is no room or reason to judge any response.

Remaining Congruent

Whether you are asking closed-ended or open-ended questions, the tone of your voice, your body language, and the way you phrase a question have a tremendous impact on others. Learning to use positive, congruent intonation and body language aids in more authentic communication.

Imagine you are standing before a dog. You lean forward, your finger pointed at his muzzle. Your voice is stern, your left hand is on your hip, and you say in a low, menacing voice, "You are such a good dog! You are the best friend I've ever had. I am so glad you're in our family."

The dog will crouch, looking sheepish and unhappy. Next you kneel down, look the dog in the eye, smile, adopt a cheerful, nice tone and say, "You are a bad, bad dog! You drive me crazy the way you track in mud. I'm not happy with you." The dog will wag its tail, lick your hand, and otherwise "smile" at you. Dogs are experts at reading nonverbal body language and voice intonation, while the verbal meaning may be lost on them.

Research has shown in all exchanges between people, most of the message is communicated nonverbally through voice intonation (31 percent), facial expression and body language (65 percent)—a total of 96 percent nonverbal! The least part—4 percent—is communicated verbally through words (Mehrabian & Weiner 1967; Philpott 1983). Nonverbal cues should confirm the verbal messages they accompany. If they contradict the words spoken then the communication becomes incongruent, and that erodes trust.

Since so much of our communication is nonverbal, it becomes necessary for coaches to observe and attune themselves to interpreting the body language of their coachees.

Imagine a teacher standing in front of a classroom. She is clutching a messy stack of papers, her posture is slouched, she looks a little unkempt, and her facial expression indicates she is tired, and maybe even bored. Students pile into the classroom, and the teacher says, "Welcome! I am glad to see you. We have an exciting lesson planned for today."

Students sense the incongruence intuitively, even if they do not recognize it cognitively. If what we say and what we do don't match, we become less believable and less effective. Why would this teacher's students participate or engage in the lesson, or even behave in class when they know she doesn't mean what she says or, if she does mean it, then she doesn't behave like she does. Beyond that, incongruence does not *feel good*. It is not a quality experience.

Whenever we communicate or interact with people, we usually have certain intentions in mind. However, sometimes our behavior does not line up with that intention. This teacher intended to conduct a good lesson with her students, yet her behavior missed the mark—she didn't convey it in her body language or voice, only in her words.

The only way she—or any of us—would recognize incongruence among our behaviors or intention comes from feedback. More than likely, she will attribute the students' response to something else, not thinking it had anything to do with her actions. Her students' behavior *may* provide the feedback that tells her the intentions she had for the lesson were not getting through. Then again, the students may not let on and she will have no way of knowing that she was incongruent and therefore not very believable.

This is another place where videotaping a lesson can be invaluable. If when questioning the teacher the coach learns her intention and the areas on which he or she wants to be coached, the coach videotapes while observing the lesson and that specific behavior. When reviewing the videotape later, the visual feedback becomes pronounced. When videotaped, the teacher should be able to see for herself how her voice, body language, and expression did or did not communicate her good intentions. The coach taped the behavior the teacher wanted to work on, and while the coach could describe the behavior and the resulting effect it had or did not have on the students, a videotape provides an even more powerful impact, particularly when the coach and the teacher view it and debrief it together.

So what if we feel like this teacher who appeared unenthusiastic. What do we do if we simply do not feel enthused? What happens if we are tired and just don't feel like being cheerful, motivating, or dynamic? What then? Well, I'll let you in on a little magic trick: *you fake it 'til you make it.* That's right. Conjure up the emotion that will serve you. Recreate the feeling of enthusiasm or excitement or anticipation of a wow experience.

As you think about what you intend to have happen, begin to get excited that it *will* happen; get enthused, and a magical thing occurs: You actually begin to feel that way! Because one's emotions tend to be reflected in the way we walk, move, or hold ourselves, our bodies will naturally respond by adopting the pose of someone enthused, excited, and motivated. You'll find yourself standing up straighter, your shoulders squared, your breathing more relaxed, a smile on your face. You're there! You're awesome! You rule!

This is not make-believe. It actually stems from work in the art and science of neurolinguistic programming (NLP—developed by researchers John Grinder and Richard Bandler in the 1970s). NLP relies on one's emotions and body language to achieve intended results. Try it sometime. You may find it's a great tool to get you through some tough times when your intention may be sound, and your behavior can't quite catch up. We'll learn more about NLP in chapter 6.

Confirmatory Paraphrases

Another important agenda skill consists of the confirmatory paraphrase. This statement paraphrases back to the one being coached what he or she said. It indicates the coach is listening, and it also allows the coach to begin using the same vocabulary and phrases that the coachee uses. Matching another's words creates trust and it also serves as a bond. The coach can get inside the head of the coachee, so to speak, using the same terminology, thus aligning further with the coachee.

The confirmatory paraphrase also indicates whether one has correctly heard and interpreted what the other person has said. If you've taken the time to frame a good open-ended question, it follows that you should listen carefully to the answer. As you actively listen, you will hear not only the words the person said but also the underlying feeling or attitude, fact, or intent. This gives a clear indication to the other person that you are listening and it also allows you to uncover the real meaning or interpretation. Also, of course, it builds a strong communication link, good rapport, and trust.

When the person being coached makes a statement, consider which of the four underlying mental states are being revealed:

- An attitude or feeling
- A fact
- An implied or expressed intent
- A commitment

Consider the following example:

"When Sarah came in late, I really got upset."

You might use the following confirmatory paraphrases to respond to that statement:

"You became angry." (Confirms attitude or feeling.)

"She is often late." (Confirms fact.)

"Next time, you want to handle the situation differently." (Confirms intent.)

"You want to handle her differently next time." (Confirms commitment.)

In most dialogues, you may wish to confirm feelings first, get the facts straight second, establish intent third, and in appropriate circumstances, establish commitment to the intention.

Once again, to determine feelings or attitude, look at the body language and listen to voice intonation. Something to note here: an attitude can be either appropriate or inappropriate; a feeling is what it is. In other words, an underlying reason exists for an attitude, yet a feeling remains just what the person feels. It's neither right nor wrong, appropriate or inappropriate. It's just what's so.

As coaches, we can flush out emotion by gently and objectively confirming what we heard (even if we "heard" it nonverbally) in order to surface what is going on. Practiced use of paraphrasing can get to an underlying attitude that may have caused the emotion, and this in turn can lead to empathetic understanding, trust, and an enhanced coaching relationship.

It's important to remember to avoid parroting back what the other person says when paraphrasing, even when you are learning to use his or her vocabulary. In other words, you don't want to say exactly the same thing; it would come across as mimicking.

Also avoid problem solving when paraphrasing. How can we solve a problem before really finding out what it consists of? The real value comes when the coach draws meaning from what was said and then paraphrases it back in a neutral statement, not in a question.

Coaches are there to confirm they heard a fact and let the other person know they heard it. They are there to confirm they picked up a feeling or attitude expressed and want to confirm that they "heard" it accurately. If they learn from the coachee that they did not hear the fact or the feeling, attitude, or intention correctly, this will give the coachee the opportunity to clarify, thus providing new information.

Examples of the introductory words in a confirmatory paraphrase that reflects fact or attitude/feeling:

"You feel . . ."
"You're saying that . . ."
"You're suggesting . . ."
"Your point is . . ."
"The problem is . . ."
"So what you're feeling is . . ."
"What I hear is . . ."
"What this says to me is . . ."
"You're saying you're frustrated about . . ."
"You're pleased that . . ."
"You want to . . ."

"You're upset about . . ."
"You're feeling vulnerable . . ."
"So what you mean to say is . . ."
"I'm hearing your exuberance and . . ."

The next example shows how using a confirmatory paraphrase (CP) can further uncover the other person's agenda:

> Coach: "What gets you excited about teaching?" (open-ended question)
>
> Teacher: "I've been thinking about teaching for a long time."
>
> Coach: "Your goal has always been to teach." (CP of fact)
>
> Teacher: "Well, no, actually, my goal was to be a social worker. I worked with low income families for several years but it was really difficult, so I decided to do something else."
>
> Coach: "You were frustrated and that led to a career change." (CP of feeling)
>
> Teacher: "Exactly. I knew there were things these families could do that they weren't doing to improve their lot in life, and one of those things was getting a good education. I decided to be a teacher to see if I could help more people become educated and improve themselves. I value education, and I wanted to make a difference, especially to low-income families."

This coach now knows a whole lot more about the coachee than just what excites her about teaching. She revealed her background, values, and motivation for teaching. The coach can focus on these values and beliefs to provide feedback that has meaning to the coachee and to guide her in maintaining her motivation and intent. Notice that the confirmatory paraphrase that missed the mark opened up the conversation to uncover the agenda.

A confirmatory paraphrase of intent restates an action to be taken. It focuses on future behavior. Confirmatory paraphrases, incidentally, provide a great tool in parent-teacher conferencing as well as in coaching situations. The key to success in using a confirmatory paraphrase of intent is to be *very* specific about the intention. "You'll try to do better next time" just isn't specific enough. You need to name the behavior or action the coachee intends.

It's also important for a coach to simply and objectively confirm the intent that was uttered, not use it as authority or it will smack of supervision. Here's an example:

You have observed a teacher coaching. You noticed three students who did not understand the lesson. From his behavior, it becomes clear the teacher was unaware this had occurred. When you tell him later about these three students, the teacher replies: "I see your point about missing those three kids." Then you could respond with your confirmatory paraphrase of intent: "Next time you will check to see that all students understand the lesson before moving on." This restates the action to be taken.

While the above example accurately depicts how to use a confirmatory paraphrase of intent, a coach may feel uncomfortable making such a statement to a colleague. Someone who possesses some authority over another generally uses it more than a peer would. A teacher might use it with students, for example.

Examples of beginnings words for confirmatory paraphrases of intent:

"Next time you . . ."

"You will . . ."

"Your intention is to . . ."

"You plan to . . ."

"Then we are in agreement that . . ."

In a coaching situation, establishing equality, trust, and avoiding even the semblance of evaluating or supervising remains important. So, in coaching, we can use a confirmatory paraphrase of *commitment*. A confirmatory paraphrase of commitment states the belief or value behind the coachee's intention. As we shall see later in this chapter, it becomes vitally important that the coach bring to the surface the coachee's beliefs, values, or visions in order to proceed in the relationship effectively. These things are an important part of the teacher's motivation and purpose behind actions and behaviors.

The confirmatory paraphrase of commitment in the above example might be stated as follows:

"It is important to you that your lesson be understood by *all* your students."

Or

"You want all students included in the learning process."

A conversation might sound like this:

Coach: "What do you hope will be the outcome of today's lesson on the election process?" (open-ended question)

Teacher: "We read and hear so much about corruption in politics that I want the kids to really appreciate how well the system does work."

Coach: "You believe in our electoral process and want to instill that knowledge in your students." (confirmatory paraphrase of commitment)

Examples of statements that lead into confirmatory paraphrases of commitment might be:

"It's important to you . . ."

"So you believe that . . ."

"You want to . . ."

"You think [feel, believe, are convinced] that . . ."

The agenda skills are also powerful to use with students, colleagues, parents, and anyone with whom you converse in your personal and professional life. With any skill, of course, practice makes perfect. As you go about your day, notice how often a closed-ended question could be changed to solicit more information. Practice rephrasing your questions as open-ended questions. When you listen to others speaking, listen for the fact, attitude, feeling, or intent behind what they say and practice paraphrasing back, confirming what you heard said and, even perhaps more importantly, what was *not* said. You will be surprised how you can enhance and strengthen communication.

Finally, if you find yourself "out of sorts," notice whether your nonverbal behavior is congruent with your intention. See if you can correct your mood by conjuring up positive emotions that will serve to focus on what you really want and intend to do—your vision.

VISION, MISSION, BELIEFS, VALUES

Most people in the field of education gravitated there because they had a vision or a belief about improving the lives of students, making a difference, imparting knowledge to others. Time, circumstances, and the maze of bureaucratic mandates and protocols can erode these visions and beliefs, and educators begin teaching only the curriculum instead of from their beliefs and vision of learning. They begin to lose their power, freedom, and fun, as described by William Glasser, M.D., in *The Quality School: Managing Students without Coercion,* discussed in chapter 3. They simply survive in the company of others whose visions were blunted in the BMW Club—the Bitching, Moaning, and Whining Club.

Nobody likes being in the BMW Club, yet once people become dues-paying members, peer pressure and agreement keep them locked in the clubhouse. They are in a comfort zone. Probably the most important aspect of a coaching program resides in the opportunity it provides to rekindle the vision of educators—to release them from the BMW Club and empower them to, once again, teach with their vision, allowing their mission, their beliefs, and their values to drive every decision.

Including a coaching program in your school creates a culture where it becomes socially unacceptable to belong to the BMW Club, like smoking cigarettes in the building, as indicated in figure 4.2.

Those who insist on remaining in the club need to be sent outside, as smokers are often asked to do. Beginning teachers may be susceptible to recruitment by the club, because they are anxious to belong. With coaching, teachers are recruited to join a different club that brings power, freedom, and fun to their professional lives.

Nothing can take away the power of a teacher who touches the lives of kids. Good teachers—great teachers—survive different testing requirements, standards, governors, post-Columbine paranoia, parents, and green-haired kids. They continue in their greatness because they are focused on their vision. They are empowered individuals making a difference!

Figure 4.2.   Ban the BMW Club

So what constitutes this vision, mission, belief, or value that we are trying to discover in a coaching session? A newspaper editorial I read some time ago cautioned readers that when discussing and deciding upon political issues, they must consider whether what they are discussing resides at the level of *vision*, *strategy*, *tactics*, or *operations*. I've always felt the same applied to teaching. The editorial "A Guide for Assessing Public Issues: Remember to Do it on Four Levels" was written by Charles Resse (1986) in *The Orlando Sentinel* and provides the following definition:

> At the level of *vision*, we are simply creating in our imagination the end result. *Stategy* involves a broad plan on how to achieve it. *Tactics* involve plans to achieve particular parts of the overall goal. *Operations* involve the execution of the tactics. (p. A10)

This same view of the various levels of a situation applies to teaching and thus to the coaching of teachers.

- If schools are to be successful in achieving their missions relating to society and the education of students, there must be agreement among school personnel—at the administrative and instructional levels—as to the mission or *vision* of the school system. The vision contains the imagined end result.
- When coaching at the level of *strategy*, we're referring to the broader plan and how to achieve it. In education, this may include how a teacher could respond to a recently adopted board-of-education curriculum or state mandated course of study. Coaching here provides the teacher with a roadmap to incorporate the strategy yet also remain true to the teacher's vision.
- *Tactics* are analogous to a lesson plan that attempts to achieve a small goal related to the overall strategy.
- *Operations* include the teacher's teaching skills and behaviors used to execute the lesson plan.

Empowering Questions: Creative, Evaluative, Personalized

To accomplish this, the coach must be skilled with open-ended questions and confirmatory paraphrases. He or she must also ask empowering questions. (See figure 5.1 in the next chapter, page 88.) These are creative, evaluative, and personalized questions, and not necessarily in that order. The way to uncover a teacher's creativity is to ask questions that elicit his or her creativity. Likewise, questions that are formed to elicit what the teacher values are evaluative questions. If the teacher and coach have had prior sessions, personalized questions can be introduced.

All questioning moves and shifts depending on the answers received, so the questioning might start by eliciting a teacher's creativity and shift as he or she says what is valued.

Creative questions allow the teacher to move away from the immediate and into his or her imagination, creativity, in order to generate ideas. They might include the following:

"Share some ideas you have considered for this lesson."

"What do you think would happen if you . . . ?"

"What other options do you have?"

"Where will your creativity show in this lesson?"

"If you could wave a magic wand over your classroom before this lesson began, what would you have the wand do?"

Evaluative questions encourage the teacher to respond based on his or her values rather than intellect. Here the coach digs for the underlying belief, value, or mission the teacher carries. The question may often be followed by a "why" to uncover the value behind the answer.

"If you were to hire your replacement, what three traits would be most important for that individual to possess?"

"How does this behavior fit with your beliefs?"

"How do you think the lesson went today?" "Why?"

"Judging from the students' responses, how do you think the lesson was received?"

Personalized questions indicate that the coach has been listening. They may be based on responses the teacher made previously.

"You said before that you appreciated humor in your students. What did you discover about that today?"

"I remember what you said about working in your previous district, and you seem to like it better here. What are the differences to you now?"

One word of caution about personalized questions: Coaches should avoid dropping into the role of friend. A friend may make assumptions in favor of, and certainly will back, a friend, whether it helps or not. A coach personalizes the question based on past conversations and events with the focus still on moving the coachee toward achieving success. Personalized questions when appropriate can help reveal more about what the coach thinks and feels. They can also underscore the trust and serve as a nudge to continue to stretch and improve.

So how does one develop good creative, evaluative, or personalized questions or statements? Typically, using open-ended questions improves the chances of eliciting those thought processes, although that is not always the case. Beyond that, the coach can use cue words that trigger a certain way of thinking. These cue words signal to the coachee what kind of thinking or what emotion is called for.

Cue Words for Creative Questions

Examples of cue words for creative questions include what I call "idea" words. Here are examples with the idea cue word italicized in each question:

Ideas—"What other *ideas* have you had?"
Goals—"And your overall *goal* in this lesson is . . ."
Options—"What are your *options* here?"
Changes—"Describe *changes* you want to make."
Ways—"In what *ways* can you improve this lesson?"
Possibilities—"What other *possibilities* might we look at?"
Opportunities—"This may lead to a lot of *opportunities*. Let's explore that."

The cue words to elicit creativity might also be couched in prediction, so the questions might contain predictive cue words:

Predict—"*Predict* the outcome of your meeting with Dan."
Hypothesize—"If you reorganized the lesson this way, what would *happen*?"
Consequences—"What are the *consequences* of doing the homework assignment first?"
Affect—"In what ways would this strategy *affect* your students?"
Effect—"What might be the *effect* on your career?"
Happen—"What would *happen* if . . . ?"

Or your questions may contain words that imply action:

Apply—"How would you *apply* this to your personal life?"
Build—"Let's *build* on that idea."
Design—"Can you show me a *design* that allows more kids to see it?"
Compose—"What could you *write* that would give you what you want?"
Create—"How will you *create* this?"
Produce—"How could this be *produced* differently?"
Build—"What else can you *build* into this?"

Cue Words for Evaluative Questions

Examples of cue words that elicit a coachee's evaluation of the situation:

Evaluate—"As you *evaluate* the situation, how did you think it went?"
Value—"What do you *value* about this process?" "Why?"
Belief—"What *beliefs* underscore what you just told me?"
Opinion—"What's your *opinion*?"
Believe—"What do you *believe* was going on?"
Judge—"How would you *judge* my performance?"
Decide—"What made you *decide* to do it that way?"

Evaluative questions may also include some words that involve analysis:

Analyze—"Let's *analyze* why you felt that way."
Reasons—"What were your *reasons* for changing that?"
Factors—"What *factors* influenced your decision to do this?"

Other ways to elicit what the coachee values may have to do with in-sight cue words:

Insights—"What *thoughts* or *insights* did you have about that issue?"
Inference—"What did you *infer* from his remark?"
Connection—"What *connections* would you make between this situation and the last?"

Cue Words and Phrases for Personalized Questions

Personalized questions reflect back to what was already discussed. Some phrases that draw on recollection are as follows:

"*Remember* when we . . . ?"
"The *last time* we discussed this, you said . . ."
"In our *last* coaching session, you were trying to . . ."

Phrases that show the coach understands the person:

"Your *strength* has always been . . ."
"I know *you feel* strongly that . . ."
"Well, I know *you value that*, so it makes sense to me that . . ."

Without getting bogged down in semantics, know that using these cue words is an excellent way to frame a question or statement to help the coachee focus on what is being sought. The point is for the coach to guide the teacher into creative, evaluative, or personalized thought processes.

Sample Conversation

Let's peek in on a preobservation conference—the coaching session where the teacher and coach determine what they want the coach to observe in the observation phase, in the classroom, or elsewhere. This came from an actual session with Sheryl Williams, a teacher from Polk County, Florida. I am seated next to Sheryl, taking notes as she talks so that she can see what I am writing.

Notice my use of open- and closed-ended questions or paraphrasing. See if you can identify where I am seeking her values, her creativity, or where I make the question more personalized. Look for cue words that I use to elicit her thinking along certain lines. While I am still seeking her agenda—what she wants observed—my primary focus remains on developing creative, evaluative, and personalized questions to help Sheryl bring to the surface her values, vision, beliefs, and mission as a teacher.

Steve: "Hi, Sheryl. What's up?"

Sheryl: "Hey, Steve! I'm feeling very creative today. I want the kids to have fun at school. I'd like to give them a 'wow' experience!"

Steve: "What do learners having fun look like or sound like for you, Sheryl?"

Sheryl: "*Good* noise. Chatter. Sidebars, discussions. The kids coming up with their own ideas. Lots of interacting, conversation."

Steve: "Learning is occurring when there's noise in the room."

Sheryl: "It is."

Steve: "What did you want me to look into or observe?"

Sheryl: "Well, as you know, Steve, I like math lessons. I think they are interactive. I'm going to introduce graphs to my students tomorrow."

Steve: "What ideas have you had for the lesson?"

Sheryl: "The students will be given crayons, and I'll be showing them how to make graphs. They collect data from one another."

Steve: "What is your role in the lesson and what task have you given the students?"

Sheryl: "I'll give them two statements which explain x, y, and the title. They'll put it all together so everything is on the graph."

Steve: "What happens then?"

Sheryl: "I'll ask them to determine how it all fits together, what it tells them."

Steve: "You're giving them activities, then debriefing the lesson."

Sheryl: "Yes. And I want them to get a sufficient amount of practice too."

Steve: "What do you believe is important about practice?"

Sheryl: "Practice will internalize it for them. I can tell them all I want, and if they practice, they'll get it. I am a firm believer in practice."

Steve: "You value practice as much as standard teaching."

Sheryl: "Yes, I do. These kids are active, and I want them to be able to use that energy to learn."

Steve: "This sounds like a lesson designed for things you've said you like about learning: interaction, movement, and opportunities for students to help one another, practice, and inductive learning. How will you decide you have succeeded in this lesson?"

Sheryl: "Students will be able to label a graph, write two comparative statements, and walk away with an understanding of how to chart data."

Steve: "What percentage of kids will tell you you've succeeded?"

Sheryl: "100 percent."

Steve: "You're going for all of them?"

Sheryl: "That's my intention, yes."

Steve: "Good for you. What role would you like me to play?"

Sheryl: "Well, there is a student named Billy who sits in the back. He's an awesome student if I grab him and get him involved. Notice if I grab him, if he comes around, and if he brings others with him. Sometimes it's Billy's class more than mine! I want it to be my class."

Steve: "How about if I come in with a focus on Billy, jot down where you are in the activity, and notice what Billy is doing at each point? Will that work?"

Sheryl: "That'll work."

Steve: "How long should I be there?"

Sheryl: "Come in at 10:00 A.M. and stay for thirty minutes."

Steve: "Here's a chart I might use. I will bring several colored pens, take notes and change pen colors every ten minutes so you get a map of what happened when. Would that help?"

Sheryl: "That's good. Note in each section what Billy is doing, okay?"

Steve: "Will do. Tell me your goal for Billy today."

Sheryl: "Today, I'd like to have him be successful early on and be motivated by that success."

Steve: "What's your goal for Billy six months from now?"

Sheryl: "What I'd like to see Billy do is work to his potential, to get into the lesson instead of disrupting the class. He can be a great leader, negative or positive. I'd like him to be a *positive* leader. He's a smart boy and could be an A student."

Steve: "With your vision and intention, Sheryl, I'm sure he will be."

Using the creative, evaluative, and personalized questions does not have a specific recipe. Each question may be peppered with elements of other types of questions. The job of a coach is to work with the teacher's vision—to first uncover it, and then to keep focused on it so that everything the teacher does is driven from a place of greatness, excitement, and enthusiasm.

LISTENING SKILLS

The most important skill a coach can have is the ability to really listen. All the correctly worded questions make no difference at all if there is not also a listening component to go with them. Listening builds the relationship; listening allows for nuance and nonverbal communication to be "heard"; listening allows for clarity; and listening ensures trust.

The gift of empathy—being able to think someone else's thoughts and feel someone else's feelings—can be indispensable to a trusting coaching relationship. This represents the ultimate level of listening. Stephen R. Covey (1990) identifies five levels of listening in his highly acclaimed book *Seven Habits of Highly Effective People* (p. 240):

- Ignoring: making no effort to listen.
- Pretend listening: giving the appearance you are listening.
- Selective listening: hearing only the parts of the conversation that interest you.
- Attentive listening: focusing on the words being said.
- Empathic listening: listening and responding with both the heart and mind to understand the person's words, intent, and feelings.

Again, paraphrasing back what the person said in terms of fact, attitude or feeling, and intention goes a long way toward assuring the coachee that the coach was indeed listening *and* understanding.

The confirmatory paraphrase shows the coachee that the coach understands how he or she felt about what was said. When people being coached hear that their feelings were so apparent (that is, the coach paraphrased back "You are upset because . . ." or "You're feeling excited about that . . ."), it helps them temper or defuse negative feelings and accelerate positive ones.

The coach also listens to gain clarity. He or she gets additional information and an exploration of all sides of a problem or issue. A coach listens in order to check meaning by restating what the coachee said. Restating what was said also encourages the coachee to hear what he or she said and this often leads to new ideas ("So, your plan is to . . ." or "As I understand it, you plan to . . .").

The coach also listens with neutrality. There are no peaks and valleys in either body language or facial expression. This conveys to the coachee that the coach remains interested and listening, and it further encourages the person to continue talking, particularly if an open-ended question was posed.

Also, the coach listens to be able to summarize what was said, possibly with a confirmation of intention. This often serves as a springboard to further discussion, a signal to move on ("These are the three things you plan to do . . ." or "So far we have decided that . . .").

The skills of coaching mimic the skills of good teaching. These include asking questions that allow latitude for the other person to express him- or herself; designing questions that elicit one's values, beliefs, creativity, and critical thinking; remaining congruent; and paraphrasing back what was said to identify fact, feeling or attitude, and intention; and, of course, the valuable tool of active listening.

Practicing these verbal skills will make them natural and powerful. They are essential to an effective coaching program. In fact, they are essential for life.

SUMMARY

These last few chapters have laid the foundation for coaching—what it is, what it isn't, what roles people play, and what skills move the coaching relationship along. Coaching makes a profoundly powerful difference in the way people feel about themselves, whether teaching or in other professions. A coach can uncover a person's latent desires and abilities, allowing him or her to maximize life experiences.

A coach's stake remains tied to the success of the person being coached. What could be more meaningful than having someone *there* for you with a strong desire and commitment to make you a better human being, a better teacher, or a better leader? Coaching not only helps teachers or others in the immediate but helps people look at their lives in a context much longer than next month, next week, or next year. Coaching can help a teacher look at the legacy he or she will leave and how that legacy impacts students and their future. Focused on this vision, many see their lives improve.

Pretty heady stuff.

And now we'll move into the three-pronged process of coaching to give it a structure within which these powerful ideas can occur.

POSSIBLE ANSWERS FOR REPHRASING CLOSED-ENDED QUESTIONS TO OPEN-ENDED QUESTIONS:

1. "Do you think your lesson will turn out well?"
   "How do you think it will turn out?"

2. "Did you think the students were interested?"
   "What showed you they were interested?"

3. "Give me another reason."
   "For instance . . . ?"

4. "What are you going to try now?"
   "What is important about the next strategy you use?"

5. "What part would you change?"
   "What changes do you think might work here?"

6. "When does it end?"
   "Where does this lead?"

II

THE COACHING PROCESS

5

The Preobservation Conference

The purpose of a preobservation conference is for a coach to use the coaching skills outlined in chapter 4 to engage in a one-on-one conversation with the person being coached. If, as poet and author David Whyte contends, "the conversation *is* the relationship," it only makes sense for the preobservation conference to be profound, meaningful, useful, and memorable.

Why do I use the word "conference" instead of "session" or "meeting"? I use conference because the coach and the coachee are coming together to confer *about* whatever the coachee wants the coach to observe. *Webster's New World College Dictionary* (1999) says to confer means "to bring together, give, grant, bestow, compare." Two people confer about real issues, real goals, and generate an in-depth look at the coachee's behaviors, attitudes, mission, and vision. This conference may also lead to innovation and exciting changes.

Real and meaningful conversations with a purpose and a focus take more time than the usual "Hi-how-are-ya?" exchanges we hold every day. Suspended conversations, empty formulas, actually take more time in the long run. They are a waste of breath, going nowhere. In a preobservation conference, the purpose is established and the focus becomes clear. Real conversation can quickly cut to the chase, getting down to the important issues and moving along quickly, efficiently, and with quality.

Often, staff development training (in the process of peer coaching) precedes the implementation of the coaching program. I typically go to a school or district and train over three to five days on the basics of coaching, some of which I've covered in this book. One of the key elements of this training underscores the trusting relationship that exists between a coach and coachee. This relationship becomes solidified at the preobservation conference stage.

Certainly two heads are better than one when strategizing or working on a skill or issue. Beyond that, however, the coach and the coachee establish and remain certain through their initial meetings and subsequent pre- and postobservation conference sessions that the coach has the coachee's best interests at heart—the coach succeeds only when the coachee succeeds.

Honing the coachee's skills, behaviors, movements, techniques, curriculum, or other aspects of teaching becomes the focus of the relationship. The relationship creates opportunities for the coachee to share and expand the powerful success strategies at his or her disposal, whether they are apparent or latent.

The desired situation is that the coach be simply a coach. The coach does not double as an evaluator or "boss." Neither is the coach strictly a friend. The coaching relationship allows the coachee to step beyond his or her role in a job, family, or collegial relationship and into the realm of improving performance, growth, and behaviors as a human being. This occurs because the coach receives permission and has at his or her disposal the skills to guide the coachee to achieve desired goals.

Cultivating the relationship occurs over the long term, so the process should begin as it is intended to continue—conferring openly, honestly, and truthfully in a safe and supportive collaborative environment. The timing and nature of the coaching sessions can vary. The preobservation conference, for example, can be via telephone, meeting place, e-mail, a casual at-home setting, or coffee shop.

A large part of the training I conduct on coaching deals with how the coach and teacher can establish and work together effectively in a safe environment. But whether the coach and coachee have undergone training in coaching or not, the initial meeting of the two is best accomplished in a "getting-to-know-you" session. Thereafter, preobservation sessions focus on specific methods or behaviors the coachee wants to improve. In subsequent postobservation conferences, the coachee receives specific feedback and support on how well he or she succeeded based on what the coach observed.

NORMS AND AGREEMENTS

Ideally, for their initial meeting the coach and coachee would meet away from school in a comfortable setting and spend an hour or two simply getting to know one another. Since that's often not possible, then each pre- and postobservation conference should be used to build rapport and understanding. To do this, I recommend the coach and coachee develop norms, agreements, or guidelines for how they will work together. These norms constitute a blueprint of the relationship — subject to upgrading or scrapping, as mutually agreed — and can be referred to at various times should the coaching relationship ever go off course.

Some suggestions for norms or agreements that might be included in your coaching relationship are shown below. While some may seem redundant, they are phrased differently and are included to trigger options of your own.

- The coachee is not broken or in need of fixing.
- The coach asks the questions; the coachee has the answers.
- The power is granted to the relationship, not to the coach.
- The relationship is custom tailored to the coachee.
- The coachee is in charge; the relationship is focused on the coachee getting the results he or she wants.
- Except when expressly stated otherwise, all conversations in the coaching sessions remain private and confidential.
- The coach ensures that the coachee is always steering toward improvement, fulfillment, and success.
- The focus of the conferences is on the one being coached — the agenda comes from the coachee.
- The coach and the coachee agree to show up on time at scheduled conferences.
- Communication is open, honest, and truthful at all times.
- The coach and the coachee agree to identify a problem before trying to solve it.
- If something is not working in the coaching relationship, the coachee has the responsibility to speak about it as soon as he or she is aware of it, to keep the trust level high.

- The coachee has a responsibility to share with the coach what seems to be working well for him or her.
- The coach remains neutral, objective, and supportive.
- The coachee remains open to suggestions, changes, or improvements.
- The coach refrains from judging, evaluating, critiquing, or sharing advice or opinions unless requested by the coachee.
- The coachee agrees to do the work necessary to make changes, improvements, or to learn skills or behaviors.
- The learning and working styles of both the coach and coachee are known to each and taken into account in the coaching relationship.

There are many other agreements the coach and coachee may develop together. The point is the relationship can be defined by parameters; it should not be loose or open ended. Too often, we enter into relationships or join teams or groups with no upfront roadmaps of how they will work together. Countless unnecessary communication problems can be avoided by the simple steps of outlining the purpose, intention, and process of relating to one another before the "topics"—whatever they may be—are raised. Two of the norms mentioned above deserve further discussion.

Problems, Options, or Opportunities?

Just as people often gather together in groups or meetings without any articulated purpose, so too do people come together to solve a problem before it has been accurately identified. When a teacher feels he or she needs coaching on a certain behavior or skill, there seems to be a tendency to refer to it as a "problem." The coach and the coachee need to agree that "a problem" in fact exists and what its nature might be before moving to solve it.

Often, the perception of a "problem" means the coachee simply does not see options that are available. Gathering all the facts surrounding the situation, stepping back and looking at the big picture, or brainstorming the genesis of the "problem" or issue are all good methods to make sure what you are trying to solve or change together. Discover if it truly represents a "problem" or an opening to explore together the options or opportunities that may surface during the conversation.

Learning and Working Styles

How the coach and coachee personally take in, organize, and store new information—new learning—provides essential information in a sound coaching relationship. Just as learning styles are important to understand in students, they are equally important to understand in educators and working adults.

A teacher's preferred learning style impacts how he or she teaches. Once the coach knows the coachee's learning and working style, he or she can provide information in ways the coachee can best learn. Every style has its own set vocabulary and terminology—its own language, if you will—and the coach can mirror back the same use of language to make a further connection in the relationship.

As an example, a teacher whose preferred sensory style is auditory might use such words as "shout," "mutter," "do as you're told," "hear," "listen in," "whine," or "yell." He or she might weave in words that refer to sound words such as "clap," "bang," "clamor," or "buzz." The coach then uses similar words when communicating to reflect the teacher's style. Knowing the styles of both the coach and the coachee greatly enhances the relationship, as each can appreciate how the other perceives, organizes, learns, and communicates information.

If you have not yet had the chance to discover your own learning and working styles or those of your coach or coachee, you've come to the right place! Performance Learning Systems (PLS) has developed a unique and highly effective instrument called The Kaleidoscope Profile. This learning styles survey has been used successfully by hundreds of thousands of students, educators, administrators, and other professionals in the workplace.

Using the Educator version of the profile (there are two versions for students, one for educators, and one for adults in the workplace), you can discover your learning and working styles. Typically the survey is completed using a unique folder and colorful sticker format. The survey is also available online. You can buy "seats" to take it.

However, since you are reading this book, I can give you permission to take the Educator version free online by using a code. To take the profile, follow these steps:

1. Go online to http://profile.plsweb.com
2. Using lowercase letters, enter this key code into the box provided: mg42vf

3. Press "Submit."
4. Fill out the registration form and click on "Submit Form."
5. You have reached the profile. Read the directions and begin!
6. The results will be automatically compiled, and you will be shown what the interpretation may mean to you as an educator or as a coach.

You are, of course, welcome to cruise the rest of the PLS site: www .plsweb.com.

One way to become acquainted or to start the coaching process at the first session might be sharing each other's learning style survey. This goes a long way toward closing the gap to understanding each other, kick-starting the relationship.

DISCOVERING AGENDA AND FOCUS

In chapter 4 we looked at various verbal skills a coach can use to uncover what is on the coachee's mind, to bring to the surface issues, ideas, concerns, and feelings that he or she has about specific teaching situations—in short, to find out his or her agenda. These are the skills needed in the preobservation conference. What specific behavior or technique or skills does the teacher want to focus on? What feedback does he or she want? Is it something to learn, improve, change, modify, or simply become aware of?

Beyond that, the preobservation conference serves as a forum for the coach to employ specific questioning and paraphrasing skills to delve deeper to uncover the vision, mission, beliefs, or values of the coachee. Empowering questions that elicit the teacher's creativity, evaluation, or more personalized thoughts help both the coach and teacher discover the focus the teacher wants in his or her professional career, teaching, or development.

In the preobservation conference, the coach listens, questions, paraphrases, observes congruency, and otherwise uncovers the coachee's belief system or values that, taken together, drive his or her vision. Uncovering the coachee's vision is an awesome task, yet it is crucial to guiding the coachee successfully. Uncovering the vision becomes a large part of the preobservation conference session. A vision does not double as a goal or an objective; a vision belongs in a larger state. As Peter Block (1990) declares in his book *The Empowered Manager*, a vision is the preferred future, a desirable state, an ideal situation. It is an expression of optimism despite the bureaucratic surrounding or the evidence to the contrary (pp. 102–3).

A vision comes out of a desire to be great—to move from good to great, both in teaching and in personal or professional development.

If this seems broad, it is because each coaching relationship evolves differently. What a coachee wants to know or change will be as varied as those relationships are. There will not be a sample list of questions. Each coaching session and each coaching relationship will be different. The questions are created out of what the coach hears—out of listening to the one being coached.

Look at figure 5.1. There are two goals of the preobservation conference. First, uncover the *agenda* of the teacher. Questions are designed to bring out the teacher's vision or belief, how that vision or belief fits with the curriculum (strategy), and how that vision or belief will be carried out in the instructional activity or lesson plan—what lesson planning and teaching skills will be used (tactics and operations).

Second, discover the *focus* for the upcoming instructional activity or lesson plan where the coach will be observing—the observation phase. The actual teaching skills (operations) that the coachee will be using constitute the focus of this stage, yet another skill set or focus could be developed, depending on the coaching relationship and situation. How the teacher operates, performs, or carries out the skill becomes the focus, and the coach observes its achievement.

In figure 5.1 the questions asked by the coach are designed to funnel down to the focus of the observation: what strategies the coachee wants to work on, the specific tactics he or she will use in a given lesson plan, and how he or she plans to use the teaching skills—how they will operate.

The focus of the observation will be driven by the first step: the coachee's agenda. As the coach discovers the teacher's driving vision or belief, he or she can better coach the teacher on the strategies and tactics based on that vision or belief. It all ties together in a way the coachee can appreciate as it meets his or her value system.

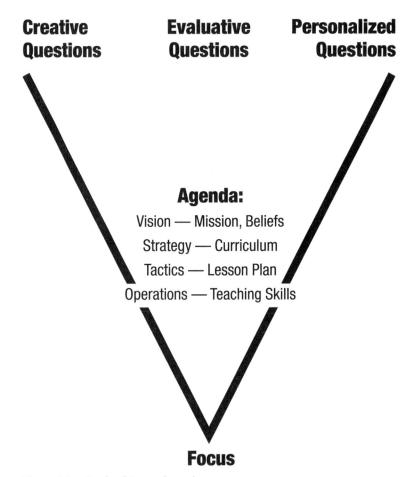

Creative Questions

Evaluative Questions

Personalized Questions

Agenda:

Vision — Mission, Beliefs

Strategy — Curriculum

Tactics — Lesson Plan

Operations — Teaching Skills

Focus

Figure 5.1.   **Goals of Preconferencing**

A coaching program at Oakwood City School District in Ohio includes teachers, principals, administrators, and some staff. Superintendent Judy Hennessey was recently coached by Debbie Smith, a computer science and journalism teacher. Debbie interviewed Judy at their preobservation session. She learned Judy was about to attend an important meeting of the Board of Trustees.

Judy wanted Debbie to observe her during the meeting and let her know if she was dominating the meeting. She was concerned she might be pushing her own agenda too adamantly, and she wanted Debbie's feedback on that particular aspect. Debbie attended this session with the board and later reported that she had gained tremendous insight into the superintendent's role and how she worked with the community to get what the district needed.

Gaining information like this provides an incidental but important offshoot of the coaching relationship. While the coach poses the questions and provides specific feedback, he or she also gains tremendous insight and knowledge about what the coachee does, feels, and envisions, even garnering some terrific strategies and lesson plans the coach can "borrow." In the example above, Debbie received the opportunity to experience the role of superintendent, something she never would have done outside a coaching relationship. More about the Oakwood coaching program appears in chapter 9.

Beginning teachers will want coaching tips and guidance from a completely different point of view than tenured teachers. If the coach also serves as principal, the angle changes again. Coaches and coachees who work in the same building will have a different relationship than those who work in separate locations.

Here is an example of a preobservation conference I held with a teacher midway through her first year of teaching. I am coaching Shelly to learn about her beliefs; notice what questions I ask to elicit them. Also notice what specific jobs she assigns me to do as her coach.

Steve: "Hi, Shelly."
Shelly: "Hi, Steve. It's good to see you again."
Steve: "Thanks. How's it going?"
Shelly: "It's going well! It's been an exciting year."
Steve: "Tell me some of the exciting parts."
Shelly: "This year the third grade teachers—and other teachers for other grades as well—started working together as a team. We have a conference planning time where we all sit down and share our ideas about what worked in our classrooms and what didn't work. We plan our lessons together so everybody can see what the other teachers are doing. That's been really effective."
Steve: "That's an ongoing, built-in coaching session you have! That's terrific. What would you say you've changed in your classroom because of the influence of working with other people on the team?"
Shelly: "One of the things I think I've changed is probably my approach to reading. Teaching reading. I've had some really good suggestions from

other teachers about how to best teach the children reading, which is one of the real problem areas in our school."

Steve: "And so you've put those suggestions to work."

Shelly: "I try to see which ones work for me and which ones don't."

Steve: "Great! One of the things that can happen with a first-year teacher is that as the year goes on, you're kind of revamping the vision that you brought into teaching. As you look back at this past year, how have you changed or modified your picture of teaching?"

Shelly: "Well, when I came in—and as an individual I'm very idealistic. I had very high goals and very high expectations. Although I didn't lower my expectations or my goals, I had to kind of adapt them to the group of people I was working with as well as the students I have. So in that way, I changed my vision a little bit. And that was kind of hard for me—to adjust to that, because I did have such high expectations."

Steve: "I love your choice of words and that you are maintaining the expectation. It may just take us a little longer to get there."

Shelly: "And I have to go about it in a different way than I had originally intended."

Steve: "Sure. That happens in a lot of cases. Now, Shelly, regarding your upcoming lesson, how would you describe the teacher's role?"

Shelly: "Well, in the lesson you're going to see the primary role of the teacher is to see if her teaching over the year has been effective—if I have taught [well how to write] a friendly letter and if my students remembered."

Steve: "So in effect, you're checking on yourself?"

Shelly: "Exactly."

Steve: "Are you going to be doing that through questions?"

Shelly: "Through questions and through student participation. They are going to use some different hands-on types of materials to show the different parts of the letter."

Steve: "Shelly, while I'm seated in the classroom watching this lesson, I will certainly observe for you everything that's happening. And, I can also zoom in and watch something in detail that I can share with you afterward."

Shelly: "That would be great."

Steve: "What might I watch in detail that I can give you specific feedback on in our postobservation conference?"

Shelly: "I think one of the things I would like to know is how I'm doing in my interactions with students on a one-on-one basis. Am I getting across my point to each individual student? Are they responding to me?"

Steve: "And how would I tell that as an observer?"

Shelly: "Maybe you could watch to see their eye contact, whether they're focusing on me, watching me; if they're participating. Sometimes you can't see if all the students are participating. Sometimes some get lost in the shuffle and you just don't see them."

Steve: "Okay. I'll pay close attention to their reactions and participation. Sounds like a good lesson."

My task is to look specifically at the students and how they focus on Shelly. When are they focused on her? What does she do to maintain that focus? I also know Shelly has a belief system built around high expectations. So I know that when I'm observing in her classroom, I want to have that mind-set and, if I want to offer a suggestion to her in the postobservation conference, it would be as to how she might maintain those high expectations. Perhaps I might give her some options for working with students.

Topics in a preobservation conference may be related to internal feelings or behavior, such as "I want to know if my underlying feelings about Erica are coming through when I call on her." Or "I'm into total burnout, and I want some feedback on ways I can rejuvenate myself and my teaching practices."

Topics may be more student or classroom specific, such as designing coherent instruction, creating effective learning activities, improving pause time and pacing of instruction, refining classroom management, etc.

Once a coaching relationship has developed to the point where there is mutual trust and assurance that each is being as open and authentic as possible, the coach can ask questions that go deeper and uncover more of the coachee's thoughts, feelings, and behaviors. I have adapted questions to education from examples used by Susan Scott in *Fierce Conversation*:

- "What has become clear since last we met?"
- "What is the area that, if you made an improvement, would give you and others the greatest benefit?"
- "What is currently impossible to do that, if it were possible, would change everything?"

- "What are you trying to make happen in the next three months?"
- "What is the most important decision you are facing?"
- "What's keeping you from making it?"
- "What topic are you hoping I won't bring up?"
- "What area under your responsibility are you most satisfied with? Least satisfied with?"
- "What part of your responsibilities are you avoiding right now?"
- "Who are your strongest students?"
- "What are you doing to ensure these students continue to be motivated?"
- "Who are your weakest students?"
- "What is your plan for these students?"
- "What conversations are you avoiding right now?"
- "What do you wish you had more time to do?"
- "What things are you doing that you would like to stop doing or delegate to someone else?"
- "If you were chosen to give input to your district, what advice would you give?"
- "What threatens you?"

CONSISTENT AND UNPREDICTABLE

It is important in a coaching relationship for the coach to be both consistent and unpredictable. Say, what? Being consistent *and* unpredictable means keeping the questions or discussions consistently in a safe environment. That is, the norms established between the coach and the coachee at the initial session are always followed. Consistent support emanates from the coach—there are no wrong answers. This support remains consistent throughout the relationship.

The unpredictable part comes from the questions themselves. The coachee will never know in advance what the questions will be or where they will lead. This keeps the coachee fresh, alert, and poised to think and feel honestly. Unpredictable questions set the foundation for coachees to reflect and to probe their thinking—ditto for students, by the way.

In an evaluation there is predictability; the teacher basically follows the map, does the expected, and can probably predict what the evaluation will say. In a coaching session, the goal is to achieve a higher order of thinking. The coach wants the coachee to stretch, to be creative, to dig for thoughts and ideas, and to share values and beliefs. Remaining consistently supportive with consistent mutual trust provides the framework within which unpredictable questions and answers synthesize to form new learning and fresh ideas.

LISTENING SKILLS REVISITED

In chapter 4 we looked at the importance of the coach having good listening skills. In a preobservation conference in particular, the coach should listen well enough to be able to complete three phrases:

"You believe that . . ."
"*My focus* when I observe you should be . . ."
"I should notice . . ."

At a minimum, the coach needs to ask and get answers to the first two phrases. Uncovering the coachee's beliefs remains a crucial part of coaching. Likewise, the focus of what the teacher wants to be coached on constitutes a key element in the coaching process.

If a coach can answer those two questions, the coach has permission to go into the classroom to observe the teacher. The two statements speak to the coachee's agenda, vision, and focus. If neither can be completed, the process of observation reverts to evaluating, not coaching.

The third phrase, "I should notice . . . ," is aimed at mentioning aspects of the coachee's behaviors or performance that are important to him or her and perhaps wouldn't get mentioned without the prompt. The teacher may want the coach to notice, for example, how he or she laughs with the students. This typically results in appreciation and gratitude on the part of the teacher.

The third phrase falls within the realm of "Well, since you *asked*, you might notice . . ." That can be anything from bulletin boards to looks on children's faces, to how professional the coachee looks in front of the classroom or in a meeting. It may also be useful to notice the way the teacher used his or her preferred learning style or how he or she rotated among learning styles to better reach all students in the class. Once again, knowing the teacher's and coach's respective learning styles can be highly useful in a coaching relationship.

I call this last phrase, the "extra credit" statement. If the coach points out something he or she noticed that is important to the coachee, good feedback results, and rapport, relationship, and trust improve. To be able to give this feedback, of course, the coach needs an understanding of the coachee's agenda and vision as established in the types of questions we have learned about already. Also, doing so shows the coach was listening.

Taking Notes

Taking notes during a preobservation conference also indicates the coach is listening, and it helps the coach note the vocabulary or terminology the coachee uses. While evaluators use words of the system, coaches use the words of the people they are coaching. The same goes for learning and working styles.

Here's an example.

> Evaluator: "Your materials were developmentally appropriate." (This ter-minology mirrors the words of the system.)
> Coach: "You lit a flame! The kids loved it." (This mirrors words that the teacher had used in the pre-observation conference as noted by the coach.)

I often suggest that the coach and coachee sit side by side in the pre-observation conference as the coach takes notes about what the coachee wants observed. Once again, it builds trust as the teacher can see exactly what the coach is planning on recording during the observation. There is no mystery.

Sometimes the coach draws a diagram if the teacher wants a record of her movements around the room or the pattern of calling on students. The coach may also use a flow chart, indicating what the coachee says he or she wants to cover at various point in a lesson. Or the coach may simply take notes during the preobservation conference reflecting what the teacher is saying so the coach knows the focus of the upcoming observation.

Another coaching model that improves the preobservation conference is shown in the next chapter, figure 6.2—an equilateral triangle with the word "content" on one line, "theory" on another, and "skills/practice" on the third. The sides of the triangle represent three general teaching areas that are not necessarily as equal in reality as the triangle suggests. In fact, sometimes they are greatly skewed. The coach and coachee can look at the triangle and together decide which of the three areas may fall within the teacher's strengths. For instance, the teacher may know the content perfectly without being totally confident in teaching theories; or the teacher may have a great deal of classroom skills practice but not be confident in subject and content areas.

Identifying the "long" and "short sides" of the triangle for the coachee ahead of the conference is useful. As we shall see in chapter 7, this triangle gives coaches a model from which they can work in the postobservation conference after having observed the teacher in action.

PREOBSERVATION CONFERENCE: REAL-LIFE EXAMPLE

To gain a picture of what a preobservation conference looks and sounds like, I'd like to walk you through a coaching situation that occurred in Cranford High School in Cranford, New Jersey. This example is interesting because the coach and the coachee switched roles back and forth, each serving as each other's coach. This is not uncommon, and the relationship evolved naturally, partly due to the shared interests of the two.

While this example involves high school teachers, the same process would apply to elementary school teachers, principals, administrators, or any others in a coaching program. Questions elicit information on which action is taken. Only the types of questions and the answers that drive the action vary from one coaching relationship to another.

Barbara Carroll is a language arts supervisor and an English teacher at Cranford High School, a suburban school with approximately a thousand students. She has taught for twenty-six years and has been a supervisor for seven. Barbara is coaching Karen Bailin, also an English teacher, having taught for twenty-eight years. Karen came to see Barbara at their designated time, and the conference went something like this:

> Barbara: "Hi Karen. How are you today?"
> Karen: "I'm great. I had a full week with lots of projects both at school and at home. That's been great, except I am completely bogged down with paperwork, Barbara."

Barbara: "You're feeling a little overwhelmed with the administrative side of teaching."

Karen: "It's not so much the administrative paperwork required by the principal or district. That's actually doable. It's the inordinate amount of paperwork generated for and from the students. I have essays to grade, questions to write. I also write up study or focus questions as I read the books they're required to read. I just feel swamped in paper."

Barbara: "Yes, that's a department-wide issue. I completely understand your feelings. I have twenty-seven students of my own, and I think I'm pushing papers more than teaching."

Karen: "That's exactly how I feel. I know the test questions and grading have to go on, and I just find that too much of my time is taken up in that."

Barbara: "What options do you have?"

Karen: "I actually wondered if the students couldn't do some of this themselves!"

Barbara: "You want the students to take over some of the paperwork."

Karen: "Well, either that, or have fewer essays or fewer questions or tests."

Barbara: "The essays you put together are valuable, Karen, and I know you believe they are terrific teaching tools that elicit quality answers."

Karen: "Yes, that's true. So what about having the students do some of the grading or questions—not their own papers, but others in the class."

Barbara: "In what ways would that impact your teaching?"

Karen: "It would free me up."

Barbara: "You'd have more free time to . . ."

Karen: "I'd have time to be innovative, Barbara. I don't feel like I have the time to be creative, innovative, come up with new and important work for the students because I'm too busy with paperwork."

Barbara: "From what I'm hearing, your issue is not so much that you feel there is too much paperwork, but that the paperwork has taken precedence over your ability to innovate—to be the creative teacher I know you want to be."

Karen: "Exactly!"

Barbara: "How do you see this evolving then?"

Karen: "Well, we have to read a book or two in class. I wondered if I could group the students and have one or two be responsible for coming up with a quiz for the others—maybe one student does it for one chapter, and one for another, and so forth."

Barbara: "You'd delegate some of the questions and quizzes to your students."

Karen: "Yes, and they could also grade each other's quizzes. That would take a lot off me."

Barbara: "My students are seniors in Advanced Placement, as you know, and I could readily see the possibilities in my class. Your students are juniors in an enriched class, and I wonder if you can predict how this might go over with your class."

Karen: "I haven't ironed out all the details, obviously, since we just came up with this. Yet I think it has merit, don't you?"

Barbara: "What's your feeling about it?"

Karen: "I'm excited. I think it has merit. They might learn a tremendous amount from one another, and in the process allow me to probe deeper, provide more insights as they move along. We just need to come up with a clear-cut plan."

Barbara: "You want me to design this with you."

Karen: "Yes. And maybe we do it with your class first, Barbara. You have a point about your students being more advanced. If it flubs in your class, there would not be as much damage as there would be in mine."

Barbara: "What makes you feel that way?"

Karen: "Your students would work with this as an interesting experiment in how to cover the trends or points in a book. They might lend some excellent ideas to our design once we come up with it."

Barbara: "You're afraid your students won't be ready."

Karen: "I think they would go for it. I just want you to try it out first!"

Barbara: "The idea is an excellent one, Karen. I'm willing to have my class try it out first. Would that make you feel more confident trying it out in your class?"

Karen: "Definitely. I would like your help and your ideas in developing the lesson design. Then we'll see how it works with your class, tweak the design a little, and try it in mine."

Barbara: "How will we know it is working?"

Karen: "How about I coach you while you deliver it. I'll observe your class, serve as your coach on this lesson. What do you think of that?"

Barbara: "It's fine with me!"

Karen: "Great! Let's do this: I'll map out what I have in conceptual form about breaking the students into groups, how they will develop questions for quizzes and some method of grading. Then let's get together and work out the details so we can begin with your class by the end of the month. How does that sound?"

Barbara: "Sounds great. I'll be thinking of ideas as well. I know your class will be reading *Brave New World*. I'm ambitious this year and hope to cover three books, so this may be a way to do that. And you'll have to take three books into account when you come up with your ideas. Me too."

Karen: "Okay. And I think the system works either way. When shall we meet for our preobservation conference?"

Barbara intended to have her AP students read and discuss Joseph Heller's *Catch-22,* Ken Kesey's *One Flew over the Cuckoo's Nest,* and Margaret Atwood's *A Hand Maid's Tale.* Barbara and Karen came up with a plan whereby students in Barbara's class were divided into three groups. The books were read and studied by each group, one at a time—that is, each group studied the same book at the same time before moving on.

Within each group, two or three students were responsible for covering a specific section of the book—say, three chapters. These students developed a quiz for the other students in the group to take before they began to make sure that each had finished the chapters by the due date. Barbara reviewed the quizzes they developed ahead of time—a day or two before the class.

One group was assigned the task of modeling how and what they were going to discuss in their group. They made their presentation to the rest of the class before the discussions began. The core group of students—two or three per group—introduced the topic that they intended to cover that day to their group, and the rest of the class could hear what they were going to be doing.

Barbara would give these students some ideas to model the kinds of discussion questions that would generate discussion, but otherwise the students came up with the topics. Some included discussing a character or characters; others used the theme of reality versus illusion in their section of the book; still others asked their group to identify three main ideas of the book to discuss as a group.

The same two or three students who developed the quizzes would lead the discussion, facilitating it so that all participated. These students would be graded on the quality of the quizzes they developed, the discussion questions they generated, how well they led the group discussion, and how they graded the quizzes, which they took home with them.

Every student in the class would have a chance to perform the role of facilitating the group discussion, including development of quizzes, discussion questions, and grading papers. The groups rotated the presentation of what they would be discussing to the rest of the class.

Barbara and Karen agreed it would be important to model this lesson to the class before they formed the groups and began the process. Because the students were divided into groups with a core team of students taking over several chapters at a time, the student should be able to cover three books in the same amount of time as one. Barbara would monitor the quizzes, questions, and graded papers, but otherwise the students were on their own.

It occurred to Karen and Barbara as they worked on this design that the students who were not "working" on preparing lessons, quizzes, discussion questions, etc., could read for pleasure. While students developing the discussion questions and quizzes would be making notes, identifying themes, and otherwise reading their sections of the book as the teacher might, the others could simply enjoy the book and await the discussion questions and quizzes developed by their fellow students.

As an added bonus, had Barbara decided to teach all three books, she would have had to do the prep work for all three. That would have created a lot of paperwork.

Barbara and Karen are experienced teachers and coaches. That is what made them readily able to collaborate on problem solving in their pre-observation conference—they've done this before. More often, when coaches start out, the preobservation conference serves to uncover the agenda and focus of the person being coached—period. That is perfectly acceptable. The coachee may have as a focus reaching all learning styles, and the agenda may be to have the coach count the times the teacher rotated the style. Working out a problem about that issue would not typically be part of this type of discussion, as the focus is specific and can be readily noticed in the observation. From that, any "problems" can be defined and discussed.

Problem solving often occurs in a postobservation conference, which in turn morphs into a new *pre*observation conference. In other words, once a problem is identified in the observation and discussed in the post-observation conference, the coachee may ask the coach to observe a specific teaching skill in the *next* observation that might rectify the initial problem. This has now become a new preobservation conference. Another observation occurs, and in the postobservation they see how everything is moving along, improving, being resolved, or perhaps requiring more work. Coaching, in short, evolves into an ongoing process of discovery, discussion, and improvement. The bottom line—it's a far cry from straight supervision.

In chapter 6, we'll see how Barbara and Karen's lesson played out during the observation of the lesson. For now, know that the preobservation conference is where coach and teacher can home in on exactly what the teacher wants to accomplish and what he or she wants the coach to observe.

SUMMARY

Questioning skills used in the preobservation conference elicit the value, focus, beliefs, and mission of the teacher as well as the specific agenda for a lesson plan, behavior, discipline issue, or any other facet of teaching. The preobservation conference can also serve to problem-solve, develop creative ideas, synthesize thoughts that result in innovation to motivate, share, grow, and raise the bar in professional teaching.

Setting norms from the get-go helps solidify the relationship, particularly the trust level. Working to identify a problem before trying to solve it goes a long way toward surfacing the real issue at hand. Note that in Barbara and Karen's case the "problem" was "too much paperwork." Yet as Barbara probed further in her role as coach, it turned out the real problem was Karen's frustration at not being able to use her creativity and innovation.

A coach who remains consistently supportive, consistent with the norms established, and consistent in the approach taken to uncover the teacher's agenda becomes free to be unpredictable in questioning. As we have seen in the examples, this unpredictability leads to refreshing ideas, new thought processes—what Oprah Winfrey calls "hallelujah moments."

Let's move to the "performance" now, the actual observation of a teacher teaching, an administrator facilitating a meeting, a coachee building confidence, or any of the myriad events that coaches can observe and on which they can provide feedback.

6

The Observation

OBSERVATION: A REAL-LIFE EXAMPLE

Room 672 houses an Advanced Placement English class on the second floor of Cranford High School. The room is cheerful and brightly decorated with colorful posters. One poster shows actor Jack Nicholson in an advertisement for the 1975 film *One Flew over the Cuckoo's Nest*. There are military objects posted on the bulletin board reflecting the atmosphere of Joseph Heller's novel *Catch-22*. Hand-drawn posters on the wall depict scenes from Margaret Atwood's novel *A Hand Maid's Tale*.

These decorations replicate the work students accomplished as they studied the three novels during the school year. On this particular day, they are prepped to complete their work on the third novel, *One Flew over the Cuckoo's Nest*.

A group of students—Group A—is seated in a circle at the front of the room, facing the remainder of the class. The teacher, Barbara Carroll, stands at the blackboard behind Group A. Her coach, Karen Bailin, has located herself in a straight chair at the back of the room. She's holding a small clipboard and pen.

Michelle, a student in Group A, stands up and hands out printed quizzes to each student in the class. The students take five minutes to complete the quiz, which demonstrates they have read the assigned chapters of *One Flew over the Cuckoo's Nest*. Michelle collects the quizzes and puts them in her notebook.

Manuel, another member of Group A, stands and asks the students in the class to count off by threes. He asks that all the ones, twos, and threes, respectively, gather in groups. There is a loud clattering and scraping of desks and chairs as students group themselves into three circles, forming groups B, C, and D.

Michelle and Manuel then outline to the students the topics they intend to cover in their section of the book. Michelle and Manuel, as part of Group A, previously developed the quizzes and read the section of the book they were asking the others to read. They collaborated and developed three discussion questions to pose to the other groups: reality versus illusion, a specific character, and three main ideas in the section. To begin the process Michelle asks the other groups to discuss the question of "reality versus illusion" as it arises in the section read. Manuel asks one person in each group to volunteer to be recorder and note what ideas its group develops on the topic in order to report to the rest of the class when the discussion is completed.

Michelle hands out the question about reality and illusion to all four groups, and the discussions within each group begin.

The teacher, Barbara, had previously approved the quiz and the discussion questions developed by Michelle and Manuel. She moves around the room listening to the discussions, making herself available should questions or confusion arise.

Her coach, Karen Bailin, also moves around the room, trying to discern whether or not the students are delving into the topic sufficiently, whether the question posed elicits commentary that shows reading comprehension, and how much the students seem to be learning. She notes which students are actively participating and which remain quiet. Karen notices crossover discussions: A student from Group B overhears comments from Group C and introduces them in Group B's discussion.

At one point, Karen and Barbara look at one another and smile. The room brims with lively discussion, excitement, and enthusiasm. Students are engaged and motivated.

After engaging in their group discussion, members of Group A stand to bring the class back to order. They call on each of the recorders from Groups B, C, and D to hear what they discussed regarding reality and illusion. Following these reports, Michelle and Manuel move to the next topic to be discussed, a specific character, and the process begins again.

By all accounts, the reading project Barbara and her coach Karen discussed in many preobservation conferences (and that we "heard" in chapter 5) appears to have paid off. Paperwork was reduced; that goal was met. Karen observed Barbara in the classroom, and the excitement and high level of learning and participation by the students delving into three different books in new and innovative ways showed Barbara the freedom that release from paperwork had given all of them.

How well had the students learned? Karen's observations and the feedback Barbara received from her, as well as the written reflections that students submitted to her at her request, will be discovered in chapter 7, where we will move into the postobservation conference. The above scene, however, highlights what the observation process might look and sound like based on Barbara and Karen's initial coaching session and the ideas generated by it.

We looked previously at the important differences among evaluators, supervisors, and peer coaches. Central to those differences are the trust and knowledge a coach has about when, how, where, and why to observe a coachee, whether in a classroom, meeting, or client presentation. As we have said before, in a school setting if a "coach" walks in to observe a classroom unannounced and uninvited, it's not coaching. It's evaluation or supervision.

EXPERTISE OF COACHES

Considering the level of expertise on a continuum (see figure 6.1), a coach who serves as an observer only—what I call "eyes, ears, and skin"—resides on one end. A coach with specific expertise on what the teacher desires coaching upon resides at the opposite end of the continuum. Both are experts.

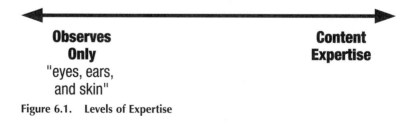

Observes Only "eyes, ears, and skin"   **Content Expertise**

Figure 6.1.   Levels of Expertise

One is an expert at observing and collecting the data the teacher requested. The other may provide expertise beyond content, such as classroom management skills or cooperative learning techniques. As an example, a twenty-year veteran teacher may serve as coach to a beginning teacher with specific areas of expertise.

I once served as an "eyes, ears, and skin" observation-only coach. I was asked to coach a teacher delivering her lesson entirely in French. She asked that I note which of the students responded to her queries and how often. I sat at the back of the classroom with a layout of the classroom and ticked off which students responded and how often they did so. Not knowing a word of French, I had no idea what the students said or whether the technique was effective. I was simply "eyes, ears, and skin" (in the sense of being present), collecting data. I really didn't need to know any more about the content than what she asked.

The coach serving as an expert on specific content or technique would go beyond simple observation. In fact, one's "regular" coach can, if need be, recommend another coach if the content is not within his or her realm of expertise and the coachee has questions about delivery of content.

In our Cranford, New Jersey, example, for instance, both teachers were English teachers. Karen was able to serve as an expert coach of Barbara's content, and vice versa. Also, Karen could coach on the content area as well as teaching strategies or student behaviors. If, however, Karen had been a math teacher, it's possible Barbara would have asked her to recommend someone else to coach that particular lesson.

CONTENT, THEORY, AND SKILLS/PRACTICE

The areas in which a teacher might want to be coached are important to uncover in the preobservation conference. Again adhering to the culture of trust, the coach would focus his or her observation on the area that the coachee wants to improve.

The equilateral triangle on page 107, figure 6.2, shows content on one side, theory on the other, and skills/practice on the bottom.

The sides of the equilateral triangle represent three general areas of teaching. Depending on a teacher's circumstances, he or she may be a whiz at classroom management and group dynamic skills (skills/practice) but lack significant knowledge in the areas of content and theory (triangle

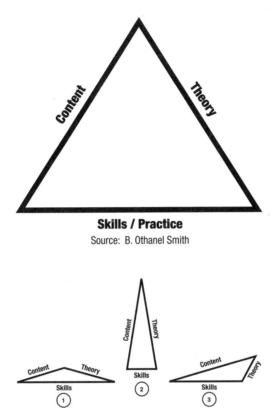

Figure 6.2. The Competent Teacher

1). Another may know much more about content and theory and less about skillfully managing a classroom (triangle 2). Still others may fall short in skills and practice and even shorter in knowledge of theory, yet know their content (triangle 3).

To build up the short side of a teacher's triangle, the coach can question the teacher in the preobservation conference, identify the teacher's strengths in the observation, and then work with him or her to improve the weaknesses in the postobservation, if that matches the coachee's wishes.

In the preobservation conference, coach and teacher identify the agenda, the focus, and also the specific ways, times, and means the teacher wishes to be coached. This can be as specific as where the teacher wants the coach to sit or stand in the room, or as broad as observing how professional the teacher appeared in general.

Often, coaches and teachers develop forms or rubrics in the pre-observation conference that the coaches will use while observing. As they sit side by side in the preobservation conference, they can together work up a worksheet that will serve them both in the observation process.

LENGTH OF AN OBSERVATION

I want to make an important point about the observation process: The frequency of observing is often more important than the length of time the coach stays in the room. I find it more effective to have a coach observe for as little as ten minutes if a teacher has a specific skill he or he is working on. The visits should be more frequent if they are to reinforce a skill. Often coaching programs get bogged down because coaches do not feel they can afford to spend an entire class period with their coachee. They need not do so. A short visit with immediate post-observation feedback is just as effective, if not more, than long visits infrequently held.

OBSERVING TEACHERS USING QUESTIONING SKILLS

In chapter 4, we looked at various questioning skills used by coaches. Teachers also employ good questioning skills in the classroom with students. Since a primary coaching skill involves asking good questions, the effectiveness with which a teacher uses questioning skills in the classroom provides an excellent focus for an observation.

Inherent in being a highly skilled coach (who is Consciously Skilled on Gordon's Ladder) is the ability to take a complex proficiency within one's area of expertise and break it down into steps so the person being coached can pick up the skills or knowledge one at a time, avoiding frustration or discouragement. This is the same process a skilled teacher uses when he or she takes a concept or proficiency and breaks it down into individual steps, through the questioning process, so students can keep up, picking up one step or bit of knowledge at a time.

One of the proficiencies used most in schools is questioning students. We ask students questions for many reasons. We want to know what they recall from what they have studied. We want to know their opinions. We want to hear their predictions and their ideas. We want to hear how they analyze and evaluate. We ask them to summarize. For these purposes we ask questions. To ask questions well, it helps to know more about the proficiency of questioning.

Asking questions is an art—an elegant art. When looking at the proficiency of questioning, we can break that proficiency into learnable skills. Just as the coach is proficient in asking questions that elicit a coachee's creativity, values, or personalized information, a teacher can be proficient in questioning students by asking questions in four different modes: memory, comprehension, creative, and evaluation.

Figure 6.3 indicates how this skill can be broken down from the complex to the simple through these four questioning modes. A teacher then may ask his or her coach to observe the questioning modes he or she used and track how students responded.

Using table 6.1 the coach can identify when and how often the questions asked by the teacher were memory, comprehension, creative, or evaluation.

The coach produces a map or record of the use of these questions and the responses of students while he or she is observing the teacher.

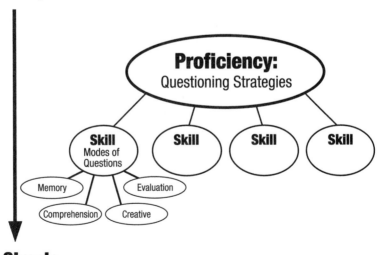

Figure 6.3. The Proficiency of Questioning

Table 6.1.   Identifying Modes of Questioning

Questioning Mode	*Thinking or Information Sought*	*When Students Answer They:*
Memory	Recognition, recall	Recall
Comprehension	Interpret, apply, analyze	Recall, use
Creative	New Ideas, solutions	Recall, use, create
Evaluation	Opinions, judgments	Recall, use, decide why

Student Answers, Teacher Responses

A teacher might also want to improve how he or she responds to student answers. There are four basic methods of responding to a student's answer. A teacher can: praise, accept, remediate, or criticize.

Here again, the coach can observe how often the teacher responds in each way and what reactions he or she receives from the students. Recording student reactions in an observation is an important part of the observation process. While coachees teaching alone may be aware of how often they respond with praise or criticism or anything in between, coaches can observe students' reactions. Often the teacher moves on to the next task, question, or response without acknowledging internally or externally the affect the question had on the student. The coach's eye can linger longer and pick up the nonverbal feedback from the student, make a note of it, and share that data with the teacher. Here is an example:

A teacher poses a question in a math lesson. The question posed is a memory question: "Students, how many quarts are in a gallon?"

Hands are raised; the teacher pauses appropriately and calls on Frances, who eagerly says, "Six!"

The teacher pauses another second and then responds to Frances by saying, "Now, Frances. You remember when we talked about this yesterday? Think again and see if you can't come up with the correct answer."

Frances is silent, staring straight ahead.

"Anyone else?" asks the teacher. "George?"

George responds correctly with "Four."

"Very good, George!"

The coach is observing the teacher's body language, the way she questions, and the facial expressions and body language of Frances and George. The coach notices that Frances appears embarrassed and George looks smug. The coach notes these for later feedback.

Table 6.2. Sample Response Chart

Teacher Response to Student Answer	Frequency
Praise	4
Acceptance	15
Remediation	10
Criticism	6

The summary of the interaction between students and teacher, while valuable to the teacher being coached, remains nonetheless subjective, as the coach interprets the body language and gestures often without the benefit of the teacher's seeing the same "language." Beyond this subjective observation, which provides the teacher with good feedback, the coach might also chart the actual responses to questions posed in one class session, like the examples shown in table 6.2 and table 6.3.

Collecting data in this way provides a clear, objective look at what happened and eliminates any subjectivity. Note that one column is marked "Unsure." This means the coach was unsure about how to categorize the response; these entries merit further discussion by coach and coachee.

John Goodlad (1984) says in *A Placed Called School* that acknowledging students empowers them and builds their self-esteem. The more praise, approval, and acceptance they receive, the more likely they are to be motivated to learn (p. 108). "Learning appears to be enhanced when students understand what is expected of them, get recognition for their work, learn quickly about their errors, and receive guidance in improving their performances" (p. 112).

Certainly the student gets it wrong sometimes, and yet isn't the effort worth a modicum of praise? Here's another way the teacher in our example above might have responded to Frances' answer about the number of quarts in a gallon.

"Students, how many quarts are in a gallon?"

Table 6.3. Expanded Sample Response Chart

Praise	Accept	Remediate	Criticize	Unsure
Awesome!	Okay.	Not quite.	No.	Like we did
You've got it.	Yes.	That's close.	That's Incorrect.	yesterday.
Exactly.	Go on.	Not exactly.	Wrong answer.	
	Hmmm . . .			

Hands are raised; the teacher pauses appropriately and calls on Frances, who eagerly says, "Six!"

The teacher pauses another second and then responds to Frances by saying, "That's a good try, Frances. You're close. Can you think back to when we talked about this yesterday? There were a lot of different numbers among pints, quarters, and gallons. Can you remember how many quarts went into a gallon?"

Frances is silent, staring straight ahead.

The teacher then says, "Okay. It will come to you. Thanks for responding. Can anyone help Frances out and remember how many quarts are in a gallon? George?"

George responds correctly with "Four."

"Very good, George! Do you remember now, Frances?"

Frances smiles and slaps her forehead with her hand, as if to say, "Of course, I knew that!" The teacher laughs gently and moves on.

With practice, responding with praise and approval becomes innate. The teacher immediately looks for something to commend the student on before making a correction or moving on to another student.

If the teacher being coached wants to improve his or her response mode, he or she works with the coach in the next preobservation conference to cite a goal. The teaching is then observed, and the coach notes the frequency of responses as before. In the postobservation conference, they go over the data, and the coach can help the teacher as he or she practices reframing responses to include some form of praise or approval for the student.

Charting Answers and Responses

Another method the coach can use to chart a teacher's responses to student answers is to re-create the layout of the classroom with student names and indicate with initials the kinds of responses the teacher gave, in a way such as that shown in figure 6.4 on page 113.

This diagram not only shows the frequency by type of response but indicates to which child the teacher gave either acceptance or remediation, criticism, or praise.

Having objective data to work with, the coachee can become more consciously aware of "the numbers" as he or she responds to student answers. Reviewing this feedback with the coach, the teacher begins to see how

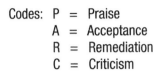

Codes: P = Praise
       A = Acceptance
       R = Remediation
       C = Criticism

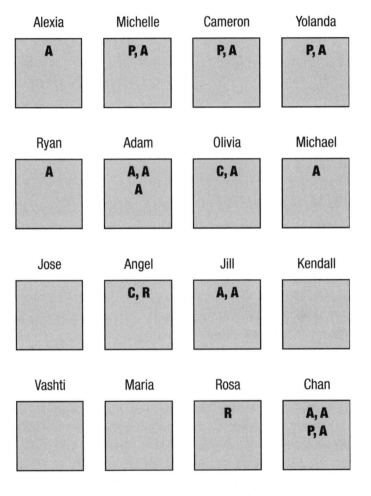

Figure 6.4. Teacher's Responses to Students

praise works to increase participation and motivation on the part of the students. This could also be readily apparent in a videotaped lesson. Having the coach collect data on the responses given only augments the empirical data.

The number of techniques, strategies, skills, designs, lessons, and professional behaviors to be coached through observation and feedback are endless. Here are a few examples of teacher behaviors that could be the topic of observation:

Gender bias
Pause periods
Modes of questions
Other biases
Use of humor
Responses to students
Nonverbal communication
Handling student behavior
Behavior in cooperative learning activities
Learning styles being reached
Multiple intelligences being reached
Strongest (and weakest) teaching styles
Congruency
Effective questioning skills
Classroom management
Experiential learning experiences
Effective lesson planning

Student behaviors and lesson characteristics are also important areas to observe. At times it is important to simply observe other teachers teaching (with no coaching involved), just to get ideas for one's own teaching, such as an observation of another special needs classroom or another English or history class. For a thorough list, see figure 6.5, Options for Observation and Coaching, on pages 115 through 119.

OPTIONS FOR OBSERVATION AND COACHING

A successful postobservation conference relies on a collection of data requested in the preobservation conference. Certainly everyone wants

The following is a partial list of options for observations and coaching. There are many more possibilities.

Teacher Behaviors

1. Gender Bias
   a. How many times do I call on males versus females?
   b. What types of questions do I ask males versus females?
   c. How many times do I offer help to males versus females?

2. Pause Periods
   a. How long do I pause before calling on a student?
   b. How long do I pause after calling on a student?
   c. How long do I pause after a student answers?

3. Modes of Questions
   a. How many times do I use memory questions versus higher-level questions?
   b. In what order do I ask various types of questions?
   c. Do I ask certain types of questions of some students and not of others?

4. Other Biases
   a. Do I show favoritism to loud versus quiet students, funny versus serious students, highly-verbal versus less-verbal students, high-achieving versus low-achieving students, etc.?
   b. Is there a difference between the way I treat students in one class period or activity and another period or activity?

5. Use of Humor
   a. Does my use of humor add or detract from my lesson? If it detracts in any way, how can I change how I use it?
   b. Is my humor tinged with sarcasm?
   c. Where in the period or lesson could I use more humor?

6. Responses to Students
   a. Which do I use the most when responding to students: praise, approval, acceptance, remediation, or criticism?
   b. Positive reinforcement: Do I give enough? Is it varied? Do I give it to all students? Does it sound sincere?

(continued)

Figure 6.5.   Options for Observation and Coaching

7. Nonverbal Communication
   a. When gesturing, how often do I use a pointing finger or an open palm?
   b. What do I do with my hands when I teach?
   c. Do I use a sarcastic tone of voice when responding to any students?
   d. To what students and areas of the room do I give eye contact?
   e. Do I move to all areas of the classroom during one class period?

8. Handling Student Behavior
   a. What could I do to better respond to _____ [student's name]?
   b. Are there things going on with students that I am not aware of?

9. Teacher Behavior During Cooperative Learning Activities
   a. Am I using appropriately sized configurations for the types of activities I assign?
   b. When I assign groups an interpersonal skill to work on, do the students understand how the skill will look and sound in their groups?
   c. Am I entering groups only when necessary?
   d. Am I allowing groups to solve their own problems?

10. Learning Styles/Intelligences
   a. What learning styles am I reaching with my presentations?
   b. What intelligences am I reaching with my presentations?
   c. What are my strongest (and weakest) teaching styles?
   d. Are there students with certain styles whom I am not reaching?

Student Behaviors

1. Focus of Attention
   a. Are students engaged in lessons? When? Which students?
   b. Are students showing signs of boredom? When? Which students?
   c. Are there things in the classroom or in my presentations which cause students to be distracted or bored?

2. Student Reactions
   a. How do students respond to my use of humor?
   b. Are there negative student responses which I am missing?
   c. Do most students seem engaged when I am making presentations?

3. Problem Students
   a. How can I respond more positively to _____ [student name]?
   b. What is a better way for me to handle the group of students in the back of the room who get off-task?

(continued)

4. Student Performance
   a. Is there something I can do to get _____ [student name] more engaged in learning?
   b. Do you see ways in which I can engage more students in this lesson?
   c. Am I doing anything which might intimidate students and keep them from responding verbally during class?
   d. Are there any students who are intimidated by other students, causing them to do less than their best?

Lesson Characteristics

1. Format
   a. What changes can I make in the order in which I present the elements of this lesson to engage more students?
   b. How is the way in which I present this lesson "turning off" students?
   c. Am I reaching my objectives with this lesson?
   d. Would it be better to demonstrate how to do_____ at the beginning or in the middle of the period?

2. Materials
   a. What visual aids could I use to enhance this lesson?
   b. What could I use that would make this lesson more real life for my students?
   c. What could I use to make this lesson more active?

3. Activities
   a. How could I turn this lesson into a simulation?
   b. How could I use role-plays to teach this material?
   c. What types of activities would get the point of this lesson across better than those I am using?
   d. I am going to try _____, which I have never done before. Please give me feedback on how well students seem to comprehend the information when I do this.

4. Sequence of Activities
   a. I want you to observe me teaching for two different class periods. I will be doing this lesson in two different ways. Give me feedback on the strengths and weaknesses of each approach.
   b. I want to reorder the activities in this lesson so students will internalize the information more quickly. What would be a better sequence for this purpose?

(*continued*)

5. Content
   a. I have taught this lesson a number of times, and students still don't seem to understand it. What could I say or do that would improve comprehension?
   b. What information could I present to students about this topic which would interest them more than what I am presenting now?
   c. What real-life activities could I use to cover the curriculum and teach life skills?

6. Pace
   a. For which students do I present my lesson too quickly? Too slowly?
   b. Where in the lesson do I need to slow down and elaborate more? Where should I speed up?

7. Assessment
   a. What could I be adding to student portfolios that would give me more information for assessing this unit?
   b. What type of rubric could I create that would help students use self-assessment during this unit?

Observations for Special Needs

1. Observe classes at your same grade level to get ideas for classroom management, how materials are presented, new activities, etc.

2. Observe classes at grade levels lower than yours to understand what content is being covered and how, before students come to you.

3. Observe someone in your same content area to get new ideas for how to present information, new activities, and new ways to review, test, assess, etc.

4. Observe teachers who are especially good at:
   a. Teaching to different learning styles/intelligences.
   b. Using visual aids.
   c. Doing live-event learning.
   d. Creating simulations.
   e. Using creative drama.
   f. Assigning portfolios.
   g. Using positive discipline.
   h. Orchestrating cooperative learning.
   i. Leading visualizations.
   j. Giving spellbinding lectures.

(*continued*)

k. Using multimedia/computers/video/the Internet.
l. Questioning techniques and Questions for Life.
m. Using specific types of activities.
n. Storytelling.
o. Employing peer-helping tools (tutoring, study buddies, etc.).
p. Group testing.
q. Conducting reviews.
r. Playing learning games.
s. Teaching life skills throughout the curriculum.
t. Teaching note-taking.
u. Employing strategies for ADD/ADHD.
v. Developing self-esteem.
w. Planning fund-raisers.
x. Teaching self-discipline and responsibility.
y. Modifying lessons for inclusion.
z. Doing creative activities.

5. Cross Curriculum/Grade Level Observations
   a. Observe a history teacher teaching about the time period in which one of your reading stories takes place.
   b. Hear what an English teacher has to say about plagiarism before assigning a term paper.
   c. Listen to a social studies teacher talk in-depth about certain current events before discussing them with your students.
   d. Have high school teachers observe elementary teachers to gain ideas for activities that add interest to lessons.
   e. Have elementary teachers observe high school teachers to see where their students are headed and what skills they are expected to have.

Adapted from "Suggestions for Peer Coaching/Observations," by Lanis Brown, Minnesota PLS instructor.

approval, and kudos such as "Good job!" or "You did fine!" are always welcome. Yet they alone are not much help to a teacher wanting to improve a specific skill. A combination of empirical data—observing first-hand what teachers did and said and the responses they received—as well as charts or graphs showing statistically when and how they accomplished particular skills can provide substantial assistance in changing coachees' behavior.

TRACKING TEACHER AND STUDENT MOVEMENTS

Page 121, figure 6.6, shows yet another method for tracking teacher behavior. Here the coach developed a replication of the classroom and charted the teacher's physical movement, the students' movements, and the order in which each occurred. Much like a football coach's outline of the team's "plays," this chart reflects each movement, and the teacher can see graphically just what occurred and when.

Both subjective and objective feedback are reviewed in the post-observation conference. The coach reveals what he or she observed and felt, and also exactly what happened, how often, or in what order. This feedback and coaching in the postobservation conference then morphs to the next preobservation conference, which, as we will see in chapter 7, often naturally occurs.

Page 144, figure 7.1, shows a form used in the post-observation conference to provide the coachee with feedback. Since completion of the form occurs during the observation phase, it is mentioned here as a reference. Further discussion about its use is found in chapter 7.

The observation phase occurs between the pre- and postobservation conferences. The coachee's real performance, practice, self-accounting, and coaching support takes place here as the teacher goes through the paces of whatever skill, technique, strategy, or behavior he or she wants to improve.

PROFESSIONAL BEHAVIOR; CONFIDENT DEMEANOR

Having made the point that objective data is important for defining discrete skills, there is also a place in coaching for the coachee to improve his or her confidence and self-esteem. Often a teacher wonders how his or her demeanor, assurance, attitude, trust, and image come across. Certainly these are all subjective observations on the part of the coach, yet the one being coached can ask for specific feedback on how his or her behavior, attitude, or demeanor impacts others—how his or her professional image is projected and received.

A coach can be a tremendous help in transforming otherwise uncomfortable, negative, or just plain tired behaviors or attitudes into shining examples of those held by true professionals. In other professions, life coaches use a variety of techniques to assist people to achieve goals in

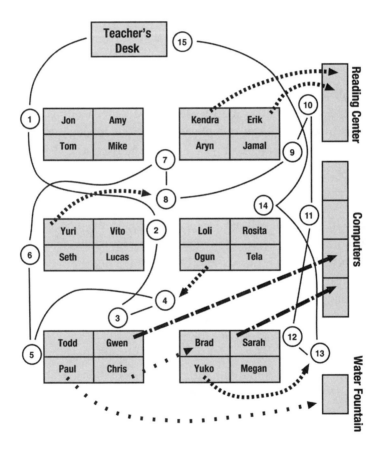

Codes:
- ━━·━━·━━▶ Students told to move
- ▪▪▪▪▪▪▪▪▪▪▶ Students move on-task
- ▪ ▪ ▪ ▪ ▪ ▶ Students move off-task
- ━━━━━━▶ Teacher movement
- (1) Teacher / student exchanges

Figure 6.6.   Tracking Classroom Movement

ways that enhance their performance in the world, attracting both people and prosperity to them naturally and with excitement and fun.

There is no reason why a teacher cannot benefit from improving his or her level of professionalism. Teachers need to feel assured they are getting the job done, that they are succeeding as professionals, that students are learning, that their ideas are well received, and that they are well respected. Teachers, like all human beings, operate at their best when they feel confident, with high self-esteem and assurance they can get the job done, that they can be trusted. Feeling this way enhances their sense of well-being and effectuality in the world.

To find ways a coach can instill this sense of confidence and well-being in another professional, we need only to look to our brains! As noted in chapter 4, John Grinder and Richard Bandler developed neuro-linguistic programming in the 1970s. It focuses on the art and science of personal excellence—a method of coding and understanding successful behavior in a way that it can be replicated. Without delving into all the aspects of this theory, some basic elements can be used to coach coachees through a process to ramp up their success.

The first element addresses physiology. Physiology means body language. It encompasses the body's stance, its structure, how we hold ourselves. In the Triune Brain Theory, developed by pioneer brain researcher Dr. Paul MacLean (1978) and reported in his article "A Mind of Three Minds: Educating the Triune Brain," there are three areas of the brain: the reptilian area, or brain stem and cerebellum; the limbic or midbrain section, containing the amygdala, hippocampus, hypothalamus, pineal gland, and thalamus; and the neomammalian section, consisting of the cerebrum and neocortex—the frontal lobe.

While problem solving, planning, and critical thinking occur in the frontal lobe, the limbic brain primarily governs emotions. MacLean's remarkable discovery was that "the limbic system, this primitive brain that can neither read nor write, provides us with the feeling of what is real, true, and important." More recent research reflected in Daniel Goleman's studies in emotional intelligence and other similar studies indicate that emotions may be more important and powerful than higher-order thinking skills when it comes to success.

So what does all this mean for coaching? Put simply, our physiology mirrors our emotions. As such, our physiology can be altered to impact emotions. As an example, if your body is slumped over, head in hand, brow creased in worry, that reflects and also generates a certain internal emotion. In contrast, you can stand straight, shoulders broad, feet planted on floor, head up, a smile on your face, a laugh emanating from your mouth. That behavior reflects and also generates a different emotion. Add to that whatever we are saying to others or to ourselves—the words we choose and our voice intonation—and we add another layer that reflects or generates emotions.

Our emotions influence our actions—we'll act one way in the slumped mode and another in the standing, smiling mode. Of course, whatever actions we take lead to results or achievement of the goals we established in our intellectual, frontal lobe of the brain.

The coach assists a coachee who wants a certain result by monitoring the coachee's body language, the emotion it reflects and generates, and therefore the action taken. This can certainly happen if the coach has brought to the surface the coachee's vision and focus. If a coachee wants to achieve a certain outcome or result in his or her presentation, the coach can assist him or her by walking through steps that rely on body movement, choice of words, and what the teacher believes about his or her abilities. That is the foundation on which the emotions that will best serve the desires of the teacher will surface.

The Story of Ned

Let's look at an example to see how this brainy stuff can work. Ned Baxter taught middle school for nine years in a semirural community. He was a good teacher and enjoyed his work. His wife Sally was offered a wonderful opportunity to advance her career; it would mean they would have to move to a new location, a city. Ned learned the city they would be living in had a teaching job only in an inner-city high school. They talked over their options and decided it would be worthwhile for both of them to move. Ned felt that while he had never taught high school, his skills as a teacher could easily translate.

He applied for and received the teaching job. He was unprepared for the huge differences he would find between his semirural middle school children and these more toughened high school inner-city students. They taunted him, laughed at him, were disrespectful, and barely obeyed his directions. He had never encountered this before and was at a loss as to how he could gain their respect.

Ned became intimidated, fearful. His self-esteem and confidence as a teacher was nearly shattered. He asked for and received permission to enter a coaching program at the school. His coach was Stan Johnson, a seasoned teacher and twenty-six-year veteran of the high school.

Ned and Stan spent several initial sessions getting to know one another and developing a trusting relationship. Stan then used the neurolinguistic programming theory to help Ned overcome the feelings he was having about teaching and his students, feelings that were clearly getting in the way of performing at his best.

In one session, Stan sat facing Ned, who was hunched forward with his hands clasped between his knees. His brow was furrowed and his body tense as he described a specific incident that had happened in his classroom earlier that day. His voice was weak, a little shaky, and he exuded exactly zero confidence.

Stan asked Ned to stand up. He told him to straighten his back, place his feet firmly on the floor about shoulder-distance apart. He told him to take some deep breaths and then smile, whether he felt like smiling or not. Ned did as he was told.

Then Stan asked Ned to talk about his teaching days back in the middle school. He asked him to describe the classroom, what he typically did on any given day, a lesson he conducted that was particularly powerful, or anything else he wanted to say, so long as it was a positive memory. Ned began to talk and shared—almost boasted—about what a good teacher he had been back then. He became animated, his stature grew, and he actually started feeling better.

Stan then asked him to share a successful story about his high school class, whether the situation had actually occurred or not. He told Ned to make it up if he had to, say how he might want it to be, all the while continuing to stand, relaxed, and solid. Ned again complied and found himself laughing as he made up a really preposterous story about how all the students in his class suddenly began applauding him, giving him a standing ovation.

By the end of the story, Ned actually felt happy, confident, relaxed. Stan suggested that he practice his body stance; start thinking about how he would like his class to react. He even suggested that Ned talk aloud, saying what he believed he could achieve—"my students have had a change of heart about me." "My class has come around so nicely. Everyone is now cooperating. We're actually having fun." "I'm a good teacher and they know it." "I've finally got the hang of teaching these high school kids!"

Stan's point was not that Ned needed to brainwash himself but rather to re-create in his body and his language and his emotions what it looked like, sounded like, and felt like to be confident, assured, and successful in his classroom and his teaching.

The theory is that as Ned practices the physiology and language along with a focus on the desired outcome—in short, once the brain and physiology have that performance pattern down pat—the resulting emotions will cause him to take actions to achieve his outcome. He will begin to talk to his students differently, use powerful and confident body language, say things in a different way to reflect his conviction that he is a good teacher and that he can teach these students as well.

With Stan supporting and coaching him, Ned practiced language and movement; he spoke aloud his beliefs about his abilities as a teacher, moving around the room with confidence and self-assurance. Sure, he felt silly at first. Yet he began to see it was paying off, if in no other way than in his emotional state. As his emotions improved, so too did his approach to his teaching, his students, his colleagues, and his wife. He was, as we mentioned in chapter 4, "faking it 'til he made it."

Stan observed Ned in his classroom frequently, for ten minutes or for thirty, depending on what Ned requested. As Stan watched Ned, he made notes about what he saw in Ned's body and the words Ned selected to use when teaching or giving directions. He made observations about the visual reaction his students had to Ned's confident approach. Not surprisingly, the student reaction was positive and reflective of Ned's "new" confidence as a teacher.

While this example does not speak to a specific skill or technique, what Ned really needed was some psychological coaching—someone to help him over a rough spot in his career. This kind of assistance not only helped Ned in his first year teaching in an inner-city high school but helped in the following years of his career. Whenever he found himself in an uncomfortable, unhappy state, he immediately noted his body stance. What was he doing? What could he do that would redirect the energy in his body?

What emotion would serve him best? He then adjusted his body language, began using language and vocabulary that would serve him better, and the emotion would inevitably arrive to help him into action.

Observation of another's action and behavior, especially by someone whose whole purpose is to help that person succeed, is a valuable gift. It not only helps the teacher and coach but impacts students. They can see an improved teacher and thus improve their learning. So, as you can see, a coachee can ask to be observed on any number of techniques, skills, behaviors, or attitudes.

SUMMARY

The coach is invited into the classroom or boardroom to provide feedback and support on the exact things the coachee requested. Observations need not last long. Frequency often becomes preferable to duration, as it provides more feedback and thus reinforces the practice that makes the skill or behavior naturally internalized. It may fit the schedule of the coach better. Then it's on to the next skill and the next observation.

Observation can be subjective or it can include a format that cites measurable, specific behaviors or skills. Both are of value to the person being coached, particularly since he or she articulated them to the coach in the preobservation conference. Once the coach has completed his or her observation, the teacher and coach debrief what occurred, and the cycle begins again with continued practice or with the next skill, behavior, or attitude the teacher wants to work on.

The postobservation conference, as we shall see in the next chapter, provides the forum for debriefing what was observed, and that in turn provides the steppingstone for the next preobservation conference.

7

The Postobservation Conference

The postobservation conference brings everything together. Here the coach and the coachee debrief what occurred during the observation, based on what was discussed and agreed upon in the preobservation conference.

The postobservation conference is the coach's opportunity to share with the teacher some of the observations made, to provide feedback. It is important that the postobservation conference provide encouragement and reinforcement for the teacher as well as create an opportunity to find something the two can begin to work on and improve.

A postobservation conference is quite different from an evaluation. In an evaluation, the evaluator who is reporting what he or she found is doing most of the talking. In a coaching conference, questions are designed to draw the teacher into the conversation, to encourage the teacher to do some hard thinking about what occurred and what might be improved.

Here, too, the focus expands to encompass not only the teacher's behavior or skill-set focus of the observation but also the impact on students and student learning. The primary reason for including a coaching program in a school is to improve teaching and thus improve student learning. So often, teachers focus on teaching to the extent they forget about student learning. Teaching can be

- Neat
- Orderly

- Sequential
- Managed
- Documented

A well-planned lesson delivered in a sequential and orderly manner with students tested immediately afterward indicates only that the lesson was taught well; no indication exists that students really learned it, unless there is student feedback or a query to the student's teacher the following year. Learning is often

- Messy
- Spontaneous
- Irregular
- Nonlinear
- Complex

The degree to which teaching and learning can coincide is the degree to which coaching is important. Coaches can collect the indicators that learning occurred. They can pick up the data about how a lesson or teacher behavior was received. While the coachee is busy teaching, the coach is busy observing what the students are saying, doing, feeling, and acting—and all of this is revealed to the coachee in the postobservation conference.

But revealed how? Using which skills? What if the lesson bombed? How does the coach give the appropriate feedback? How do you do that?

Well, you've come to the right place to find out.

THE COACHING ENVIRONMENT

The postobservation conference provides a safe environment within which the coach and the coachee can relax, look at what just occurred in the "performance" of teaching and learning—the observation—and to-gether work toward improving, enhancing, or celebrating what has oc-curred and will occur in the future.

In the postobservation conference, the person being coached receives feedback based on what was discussed or created in the preobservation conference. This is when the coach uses skills to guide, advance, and totally support the positive aspects of what the coachee has accomplished. Options and ideas and suggestions can certainly surface; the important piece here is to give the coachee opportunities to advance, improve, move forward based on the positive aspects of what just occurred in the observation.

The timing of the postobservation conference depends somewhat on the agenda and vision of the person being coached. The observation could be one that continues for a month or so after the preobservation conference, or it could take only one day or one section of a lesson, depending on the coachee's specific agenda. Regardless of the length of the actual observation, the postobservation conference should occur as soon as possible after the last observation in order to capture what went on and connect to the preobservation conference.

This timing is also important because the preobservation conference will have developed a relationship of trust and rapport. The building of the relationship followed a supportive observation by the coach, so it follows that the trust and rapport should be reinforced by a smooth transition into the postobservation conference. If you wait too long to hold the postobservation conference, this trust and rapport could dwindle or be lost.

Unlike coaching, an evaluation provides feedback: "This is what you did and how well you pulled it off." I like to think observation and follow-up coaching at the postobservation conference *together* allow the coach to provide feed*forward* for the coachee instead. To move the relationship and the vision forward and to make the coaching situation a safe place requires a positive environment.

A Positive Environment

The most important component of a safe coaching relationship lies in the establishment of a positive environment within which coaches can share their observations without any hint of evaluation or awkwardness on the part of coachees. While this seems obvious, it is often easier said than done. Not only does a positive environment include positive attitudes, but its focus is on success and support. This paves the way for healthy discussion, generates positive energy, requires less talking, and allows for a better focus on the task at hand. In fact, research shows that being positive is more productive than being negative.

Somehow we humans gravitate toward the negative. I use the word "gravitate" almost literally—it's almost as if negative energy mimics gravity and we need to make an effort to create a positive climate, to get buoyant, to stay erect, and moving forward. We are accustomed to a negative mental set. We see it in the news, in weaknesses in our institutions, mismanagement, and bad service. Negativity generates an unproductive and even counterproductive spiral. A positive mental set, on the other hand, produces a positive, upward spiral.

When I train professionals or students, I often use a simple exercise of writing on the board the word "Enjoy" at the top of one column and "Avoid" at the top of the other. I use a green marker to write Enjoy and red to write Avoid, reminiscent of a stoplight. People list the things they enjoy in general on one side (usually not work- or school-related activities), such as walking, traveling, cooking, golf. On the Avoid side, they often list tasks or situations that sound like punishment to them, things that have no reward, that seem never ending, such as housecleaning, doing the laundry, paying bills, preparing income taxes, etc. The reason I so strongly support and promote a coaching program in schools is that it removes some of the things we wish to avoid in the teaching profession by providing teachers with more options so their daily experience at school resembles more and more their Enjoy lists. The more enjoyment teachers have as they teach, the better they will be at reaching students, and the easier it will be to cope with those necessary items on a teacher's Avoid list.

Positive Phrasing

In addition to a positive environment, certain skills must be used while coaching to ensure that the give-and-take between coach and coachee not only remains positive but also provides feedforward and underscores the trust in the relationship. An example is the use of Positive Phrasing.

Positive Phrasing simply states something in a way that lets the other person know what you *do* want, not what you *don't* want. You focus on what you want the other person to know or do.

Here's an experiment. Don't think about the Golden Gate Bridge. Ha! Gotcha! You had that orange-painted bridge firmly suspended in your mind, didn't you? Yet I told you *not* to think of the Golden Gate Bridge. What gives?

Research reported in *Behavioral Kinesiology* by John Diamond (1979) that when you want someone to follow directions, a person will comprehend what to do 47 percent faster if you tell what to do rather than what not to do. There are two theories for why this works. They come from related theories that the right and left hemispheres of the brain have separate functions. Some scientists believe the right brain does not interpret or process negative messages. The right brain simply drops the "don't" part in a command. The direction "Don't squeeze the lemon" to the right brain means forget that "don't" part, and squeeeeeeze . . . !

A similar theory is that when the left-brain hears the command "Don't squeeze the lemon," it has to translate that into a behavior the right brain can carry out. A time lapse occurs as the brain attempts to comprehend what "don't" means. As the brain makes the translation or moves on to other stimuli, the opposite behavioral response occurs, and, yep, you guessed it, squeeeeeeze . . . !

When we rehearse events in our mind—when we visualize succeeding or performing, for example—we always focus on what we want to occur. Visualizing what we do *not* want to occur constitutes worry. While there may be some value in visualizing a worst-case scenario and then deciding to proceed anyway knowing you can handle the consequences, the primary value of visualization remains in achieving something we desire, for which we have positive emotions. It's difficult to visualize not doing something, to visualize a void.

Using Positive Phrasing in coaching serves to leave a desired behavior instilled within the mind of those being coached. You want coachees to remember what they want to do, what they should do, not what they don't want to do, or shouldn't do. You want them rehearsing the correct, positive behavior.

This is easier said than done, by the way. We are all so familiar with negative phrasing, such as "knock it off," "don't worry," "don't compare yourself to that veteran teacher," "stop thinking about how you look and concentrate on doing it right."

Let's try your hand at improving negatively phrased directions. Change the following negative coaching phrases to positive ones. Suggested answers are at the end of this chapter on page 149.

1. "Stop using outdated, messy materials."
2. "Don't look only at one side of the room when you are teaching."
3. "Don't slouch when you sit at the conference table."
4. "Stop calling only on boys when you ask a question that involves math."
5. "Don't go so fast."

Positive Phrasing consists of two steps. The first is mental—think positively. The second is to focus on what you want the other person to know and do. Positive Phrasing is a skill that can be used by itself or with other verbal skills. It has a ripple effect when used with open-ended questions, supporting statements, empathetic phrases. Positive Phrasing concentrates on the positive aspects of any situation; it looks at the glass as half full and then concentrates on filling the rest of the glass.

When a coach lends his or her ideas to a coachee about changes in behavior, the positively phrased suggestion or idea must:

- Be clear and specific
- Be congruent with the teacher's vision
- Offer some kind of payoff

By being *clear and specific*, I mean the coach has to refer to exact behavior. Saying "you handled that well" does not tell the coachee what specific thing he or she did well that constituted "handled." Instead, the Positive Phrase should be clear and specific describing the behavior: "When you asked the student to stand up, you really managed to defuse his disruptive behavior in class."

One of the reasons evaluations seldom change teacher performance is that they usually do not refer to specific behaviors. Rather, they speak in generalities. An evaluator may say to a teacher, "You need to be more positive." The teacher does not know what that means to him- or herself or to the evaluator, and neither do I. It could mean open body language, with the arms held at one's side and not folded, phrasing directions in a positive way, making pleasant eye contact, smiling—it's not clear what it means.

Second, not only is it crucial for a coach to be clear and specific, it's important that the *coach be congruent with the coachee's values and vi-*

sion. Being congruent means the idea or option the coach offers fits with what the other person values. Spending quality time in the preobservation conference uncovering the coachee's agenda allows for the coach to provide options congruent with that agenda.

Finally, the Positive Phrase needs to *offer some benefit*, some incentive for the coachee to make a change. As Dr. Phil McGraw (1999) points out in *Life Strategies: Doing What Works, Doing What Matters* and his other related books, no one does anything without perceiving some purpose or value in doing it, or what he calls "a payoff." The payoff for making a change has to be at least as great as or greater than the cost of making the change.

As we will see in chapter 8, there is a metaphorical cost in implementing coaching programs in schools or districts. People implementing the program must be convinced that the payoffs—the benefits—of coaching outweigh the costs—added time, commitment—or the program will not be implemented or successful.

Likewise, a teacher being coached to change a lesson plan that remains fun and well received by students but provides nothing more than busy-work—no substantive content is involved—must be assured that the payoff of revising the delivery merits the cost of discarding one of her favorite lessons.

Needs/Benefit Statement

A Needs/Benefit Statement employs Positive Phrasing that tells someone what you want to be known or done, and it takes it one step further. A Needs/Benefit Statement attaches a benefit that will result if the person follows through on the suggestion, the positively phrased direction. It offers a payoff in terms of improving effectiveness, replacing behaviors that don't pay off with students. The Needs/Benefit Statement shows the other person a need that will be filled by a desired action and also how he or she will benefit from that need being fulfilled. Here's the key to using it correctly: *The benefit must match the other person's agenda to be effective.*

As an example, let's say you fully understand the beliefs, values, and vision of the person you are coaching. You know that he values strong communication skills and endeavors to improve them at all times. During the observation of his teaching, you note that he is clear and precise in his delivery; his communication to the students is good. Yet his eyes remain fixed on one side of the room. He only glances occasionally at a whole group of students residing on the other side of the room.

You want to alert the teacher to this habit in a way that is both positive and motivating. Since you know he values communication, there is a built-in motivation. A suggested Needs/Benefit Statement might be: "To improve communication with all your students, Fred, practice sweeping your eyes across the entire room as you speak to them, making eye contact with each student as you do so."

As a coach, it is your job to tell coachees how they will benefit when they try new strategies. Let's try another one.

The person being coached really wants to be promoted. She has been overlooked in the past and now really wants to accelerate her career. As her coach, you observe her in a meeting, noting that she brought in a messy notebook, kept rustling through papers, fidgeting, and otherwise looked very unorganized and less than professional. At the same time, this person prides herself on her organizational skills; she just gets flustered when she attends a meeting where those who could advance her career are present. She's not at her best, nervous, trying too hard to make a good impression.

To improve her odds of getting a promotion, her "need" is to organize her materials, center herself before the meeting, and remain calm during the meeting. The "benefit" of doing so is that she will come across with more confidence and appear organized and efficient. A Needs/Benefit Statement given to her by her coach might go something like this: "Your expertise would be noticed a lot more, Becky, by showing how organized you are with your papers in order before the meeting. Some prior organization would allow you to appear calm and 'together,' even if you are still nervous about the meeting."

You may recall that in chapter 3 we looked at creative, evaluative, and personalized questions based on what the coach understood about what the coachee valued. In the same vein, a Needs/Benefit Statement can be used to reflect what the coachee values—what motivates and inspires him or her. The coach knows that because he or she learned it from questions posed in the preobservation conference.

One of the reasons a coaching program includes the preobservation conference is to give time for the coach and coachee to know one another, to uncover the coachee's agenda and focus. In the postobservation conference, the coach softly prods the coachee to perform at his or her best with needs being met and benefits realized based on what that person values.

Approval Statements

The Approval Statement deals with self-esteem. We all like to think of ourselves as having certain qualities that we can be proud of. Some people pride themselves on their creativity; others on clear thinking. One person may take particular pride in being loyal, while another may consider his or her leadership ability to be important. The number of positive attributes a person might be proud of is virtually endless, and each person has his or her own list of traits on which self-concept is built.

The key to offering an effective Approval Statement lies in using positive adjectives to describe qualities or behaviors a person values. What people value shows up in their actions and by what they produce. In an Approval Statement, positive adjectives are applied to those actions or products that the person values. For example, "That was a well-organized and stimulating lesson" includes adjectives ("well-organized" and "stimulating") relating directly to what a coachee has told the coach in a preobservation conference that he or she valued.

Here are others. Each person receiving one of these messages from his or her coach hears things they value. Note the adjectives used and italicized.

"Your *concern for children* is evident in the way you speak to them."

"Your questioning strategy was *well thought out* and *kept your students on task.*"

"Your response to the parent was *honest and authentic.*"

"Your willingness to change based on ideas generated in our last coaching session shows your *commitment to your students.*"

On page 136 you will see another list of approval adjectives, in table 7.1; each of them connects back to qualities or behaviors a person might value. What the person values shows in his or her actions and the results of those actions.

A coach provides a coachee reinforcement and feedforward when giving suggestions he or she can use in the future. This is accomplished

Table 7.1.   List of Approval Adjectives

Approval Adjectives

accurate	expressive	pleasant
achiever	flexible	polished
adaptable	fluent	polite
agreeable	forward	popular
appreciative	frank	positive
artistic	friendly	prompt
athletic	generous	realistic
attentive	gentle	relaxed
attractive	good-looking	reliable
calm	good sense of humor	responsible
capable	good mixer	responsive
careful	good-natured	self-starter
cheerful	helpful	smart
competitive	honest	soft-hearted
conscientious	humble	sophisticated
considerate	humorous	spirited
convincing	inspiring	steady
cooperative	intellectual	strong-willed
courageous	intelligent	supportive
creative	interesting	tenacious
daring	kind	thorough
dependable	leader	thoughtful
detail-oriented	likable	tolerant
direct	loyal	trailblazer
disciplined	modest	trusted
dramatic	motivated	trusting
dynamic	neat	trustworthy
eager	neighborly	understanding
easygoing	optimistic	unique
effective	organized	upbeat
efficient	outgoing	verbal
energetic	persistent	vigorous
enterprising	persuasive	vivacious

Source: *Coaching Skills for Successful Teaching*

through clear, specific, congruent, and Positive Phrasing, with a Needs/ Benefit Statements indicating a positive payoff.

If the dialogue flows, the coach will find opportunities to make a suggestion or suggestions. It will just feel right and will fit in with the flow of the conversation. Remember that trust is built by keeping the post-observation conference focused on the agenda that was established in the preobservation conference.

Feedback and encouragement are provided to the person being coached in the form of an Approval Statement. The Approval Statement reflects what the person did that was consistent with what he or she values: it worked, it clicked, bravo, keep going, do it again. It's feedback and encouragement in a positive light.

So what exactly constitutes an Approval Statement? Well, it's not a compliment, and it's not praise. A *compliment* provides positive feedback to people about their possessions, traits, or appearance. You compliment someone's car, their hair style, a mustache that flatters, someone's apparel, or one's joyful laughter. With *praise*, you provide positive feedback for what the person may have done, usually something that matches *your* idea of what's good, valuable, or important.

Approval, on the other hand, provides positive feedback for something that the other person values—what he or she considers important and worthwhile. It's important for the person giving the Approval Statement to check the reaction after delivering one to make sure the statement reflects, in fact, what the other person values. This is not easy to do in an e-mail. Body language plays a big part, so being with the person when delivering Approval Statements becomes critical.

Human behavior sports an odd reaction to compliments, praise, and even approval. People tend to brush them off, become embarrassed, or not even feel they are worthy of them. With approval, as compared to compliments and praise, you have a better chance of a person's hearing your approval because, if you've done your homework, they hear something of value to them, something that resonates.

There are certain guidelines you can use when giving Approval Statements that tend to reach the mark more effectively. First, *give approval in a sentence by itself.* A common situation arises in postobservation conferences with novice coaches. The tendency is to deliver Approval Statements along with coaching, which sounds like this: "That was *such* a creative opening to the lesson. The way you engaged your students when setting up the activity was really impressive *and* . . ." On the word "and," the coach looks down at notes in order to see what to say next and breaks eye contact. Once that happens, the coachee receiving the approval remains hanging on the word "and" rather than enjoying the authentic approval.

Said differently, after you give an Approval Statement, "shut up!" In the case above, you would say, "That was such a creative opening to the lesson" and then stop a bit before going on. Anything you add after the approval diminishes it. Let it sink in at the person's heart level. If you deliver the approval and add more, the next sentence after the approval beams them back into their brain or their intellect, and the heartfelt approval gets washed out.

Second, when delivering the Approval Statement, *maintain eye contact for several seconds afterward.* This allows the other person to hear the approval and to relate to its value, and it gives the person delivering the Approval Statement an opportunity to read how the person responds to the approval. Did it hit the mark? Did his or her eyes light up? Or did he or she look confused? Unless you let the Approval Statement hover in the air while making direct eye contact, you won't know.

Third, *read body language for reaction.* We all know body language constitutes the lion's share of communication. You can tell by people's body language whether approval met with *their* approval. There will be a big smile, a laugh, a visible relaxation of the shoulders, or other evidence of satisfaction. A frown or no reaction means you need to try something else. You have not hit on something the person values.

Fourth, *if you get a negative reaction,* whether in body language or actual comments, *give more approval,* ask a question, or use a paraphrase to learn more. Keep checking to make sure the approval speaks to coachees' values, that the approval is something they enjoy or appreciate.

Approval feeds the ego. A compliment or praise is more evaluative— it's based on someone else's opinions, values, focus. Approval also requires that the person delivering the statement really knows the one receiving approval. You can give a compliment or praise to a total stranger—not so with an Approval Statement.

By the way, the Approval Statement should coincide with your own values too, thus bonding the relationship further.

POSTOBSERVATION CONFERENCE: A REAL-LIFE EXAMPLE

In chapter 5 we witnessed a preobservation conference between beginning teacher Shelly and me. Here is how our postobservation conference played out. Notice my use of questions and approvals to engage Shelly, as well as the use of a suggestion she might take away from the post-observation conference experience.

Steve: "Shelly, you asked me to observe your students' attention or focus on you and your awareness of whether or not you engaged them."

Shelly: "Well, I hope I did. Most of them seemed to be watching me and focusing on what we were doing as well as listening to the other children around them. That's kind of how you gauge it—if they are listening to the person that came before them. So in that regard, I think they were listening and paying attention."

Steve: "It sure looked to me like you had their attention the entire time. I focused on some of the things that I thought caused that. What would you guess caused the students to be focused on you?"

Shelly: "Well, I try to use a variety of teaching methods. Some teacher-directed things. Some student interaction, hands-on materials. Those types of things, I think, helped them stay involved."

Steve: "I noted that the students had to move from their focus on you when you labeled the parts of the letter on the board, to labeling the parts on their own paper, and then back to you again. That really required each student to stay with what you were saying and doing."

Shelly: "Right. They would have to be with me to capture that."

Steve: "Do you have any other thoughts about what might cause them to be focused on you?"

Shelly: "Well, not any others, right at this moment. No."

Steve: "To what extent do you sense that you're on stage when you're teaching?"

Shelly: "Oh that's probably a large part of it. I just never think about it. You have to act out what you're doing. The more animated you are, the more focused they are."

Steve: "You have an interesting array of nonverbal communication—body language. At the beginning of the lesson when you stepped in to introduce the story, the use of your voice, your body posture, and your hand movements sent out a real stage presence. You also used your body language to encourage and clue the students. If their answers were going down the wrong path, you held an exaggerated look in your eye, or when they were getting it correctly, you had exaggerated encouragement in your smile that said loud and clear, 'You're on the right track, keep it coming.' This animated body language has a lot of use for you when focusing on your students."

Shelly: "I talk a lot with my hands! If I didn't have them, I'd probably get into trouble."

Steve: "You make it easy for students to pay attention to you."

Shelly: "Good!"

Steve: "What role do you figure your relationships with students plays in terms of keeping their focused learning attention?"

Shelly: "I think it's so important to understand each child that's in your room, to know their backgrounds and know what motivates them to want to learn. Because they don't all learn the same, and not everything motivates each student the same way. And sometimes it's hard to pick out what motivates each individual student. It's hard to always focus on that in each lesson. The more you can do that, the more likely they are to achieve."

Steve: "There was a sequence with Terrance when he gave you the wrong answer. Again, you used your body language to send a caring message out to him. Your actual response was, 'Real close. You got the S-word there.' Then you went on to another student who gave the correct answer. But it was clear to me you kept Terrance in mind, because when it was time for the answer that he gave to be the right answer, you slid back to him, and pulled him back in. That's a powerful strategy. If a student were going to leave a lesson—to stop focusing on it—it would be right after giving a wrong answer. And when an answer he or she gave is the one for another question, that is the perfect chance to come around and bring him or her back in. You did that well."

Shelly: "I try to keep it in mind. It's hard to always remember, but I did remember that time. Especially with that particular student, whom I know needs reinforcement."

Steve: "I think your whole use of names is good too. Not only using names when you call on students, but also when you come back to them. Or when you talk about their answers, there's more personalization there. One area you might want to look at for increasing student focus is on the length of time you allow after your question before you call on a student. There's a tendency on all our parts as teachers to speed on to the next student if the first one doesn't start to answer the question right away. That might be an area where you could cause more students to stay with you a little bit longer by increasing that time frame. Have you done any work with that—with pause time?"

Shelly: "No, but I've heard a lot about it. It's very hard to focus on timing. There is a tendency not to concentrate on anything except 'Okay, I've got to keep this moving, I've got to keep this going.'"

Steve: "Frequently a teacher's strengths can also get in the way. Teachers who have lots of energy, high enthusiasm, and a keen sense of state—and I would say you're that type of teacher—find that teaching has its own momentum that builds as the lesson is going on. It requires a conscious shift that may seem incongruous to pull back, slow down, and pause. It's one that all of us—even experienced teachers—need to come back and review from time to time."

Shelly: "That's good to know."

Steve: "As a matter of fact, I wouldn't mind doing some conscious practice on it myself. If you're willing, I'd like to find a time when you could come observe me making a presentation. What I'd like you to do is record my pause time for me. I think that, knowing you are in the room observing me, it would give me a chance to become more conscious of slowing down, pausing, letting the question sit for awhile. Then if you like, I'd come back and do an observation for you again."

Shelly: "That would be wonderful."

REINFORCEMENT AND ENCOURAGEMENT

Let's look at the notion of reinforcement and encouragement again. Having viewed hundreds of videotapes showing teachers teaching, I have been struck by the fact that most teachers are unable to provide their own reinforcement—to be conscious of what they are doing right. The videotape format makes their shortcomings seem larger than life, while their successful practices fly by unnoticed. If this phenomenon occurs in the videotape format, then surely even less self-reinforcement takes place in the classroom when a teacher's attention is focused on students and the delivery of a lesson.

Reinforcement of specific, effective teaching skills can make teachers conscious of their behavior in the classroom. This consciousness, in turn, increases their use of effective behaviors and adds to their level of professionalism. Teachers who do not have the benefit of coaching feedback—and are Unconsciously Talented—consider themselves just lucky, not skilled. A coach using Positive Phrasing that is clear and specific, congruent with the teacher's values, and cites a positive payoff for the teacher not only reinforces the teacher's behavior but paves the way for further improvement.

Moving from reinforcement to encouragement brings us to the next step. Encouragement searches for and accentuates the positive. It aims at helping the coachee develop self-acceptance and self-worth. Teachers—or anyone, for that matter—need to develop self-esteem before risking change or experimentation. Encouragement speaks to an individual's vision and beliefs. Coaches can provide encouragement when they understand how the teacher perceives his or her brand of teaching, both now and in the future. Recognizing, reinforcing, and encouraging a teacher increases the likelihood that new skills and behaviors will be internalized.

Sadly, encouragement in a standard evaluation process is rare, possibly because it involves a commitment to addressing the other person's needs as opposed to one's own needs or that of the system. When training administrators, mentors, department chairpersons, and coaches, I have uncovered two myths that decrease the use of reinforcement and encouragement.

Myth No. 1: Educators who have been trained to give approval to students will perceive reinforcement and encouragement from peers as being manipulative.

Many educators who hold this point of view are surprised at how satisfying they find approval to be in the context of a coaching relationship built upon trust. I have personally observed teachers "sitting tall" after several coaching colleagues created a list of reinforcing statements for them.

Myth No. 2: When professional friendships have developed over years of working together, Approval Statements are unnecessary.

I uncovered this myth after observing fifteen school administrators conduct coaching conferences with staff members with whom they had positive professional relationships. When I commented on the lack of reinforcement in the conferences, the teachers quickly defended the administrators, saying, "I don't need it," or "I know that he [or she] approves of what I did."

Administrators responded by identifying that they wanted to offer more approval and were not sure the teachers would value it (see Myth No. 1). Continued discussion revealed that both teachers and administrators would enjoy genuine approval and signs of acceptance.

As in other relationships, we assume our unspoken messages are somehow communicated. Reinforcement and Approval Statements must be plainly stated. This purposeful focus rewards both the giver and the receiver.

Here are some guidelines to assist coaches in providing effective reinforcement and encouragement while coaching:

- Communicate your enthusiasm and sincerity through your statements. Make each one a minicelebration. Intonation and body language play an important role in communicating approval so be aware of your nonverbals.
- Always think of your statements from a particular coachee's perspective. Are you reinforcing and encouraging behaviors that fit this individual's vision, beliefs, and what is valued?
- Be specific. By citing the specific occurrence you are reinforcing, you not only add value to the reinforcement, you also increase your own credibility as a knowledgeable coach.

PLANNING A POSTOBSERVATION PROCESS

Techniques that create a safe, positive environment while coaching are all focused on giving a teacher the framework he or she needs to continue to improve and grow.

On page 144 is the form I referred to in chapter 6, figure 7.1, Postobservation Conference Planning Sheet.

There are three symbols topping three columns on this form. The first is a heart, the second a question mark, and the third a blazing light bulb. These represent heartfelt approval, questions, and ideas or suggestions. When planning a postobservation conference, it is useful to plan it backward, starting with the last column. This will represent what the coach wants to convey at the end of the postobservation conference.

After observing the coachee, the coach starts at the right end of the sheet and notes first one suggestion or idea he or she has to help the teacher improve. In the preobservation conference, the teacher's agenda revealed what he or she wanted to work on—the coach and teacher together uncovered a suggestion or idea for improvement. Usually only one idea is sufficient; otherwise, the session begins to look like an evaluation.

Figure 7.1.   Postobservation Conference Planning Sheet

As teachers work on one change, it typically leads to other changes, so starting with one is not limiting in the long run.

Here is an example of how the form might be used. A coach observes that his coachee delivers his lesson from the front of the room at a rather fast pace. The coach notices that students are struggling to keep up. A suggestion for the coachee might be to add more interest in the lesson by more fluid movement around the room. Doing so would also tend to slow down the pace. The coach makes a note in the Idea column (light bulb): "Add more movement."

Next, after the coach has thought of the suggestion or idea and jotted it down, he or she looks at questions he or she could ask about the lesson or the observation around which an Approval Statement can be formed. In an example I gave earlier, the teacher stationed himself in one spot in the room. The question the coach came up with focuses on his reason for doing that: "What is your thinking about the way you have the room arranged? In an ideal situation, what would you prefer?" So the coach jots questions down under the question mark on the form.

The coach knows this teacher *values* being as dynamic and interesting as possible. So the question then leads to what he might write in the first column, the Approval Statement (the heart). "When you walked over to the map and helped students locate the country, you were really engaging their interest." "Your use of space in the room was very powerful as you went around assigning each student a country to work on."

While the heart/question mark/light bulb form is filled in backward when planning a conference (right to left), when delivering the postobservation conference, the Approval Statement is delivered first in the postobservation conference. The form is used the way it is sequenced.

In the example involving Ned Baxter in chapter 6, the teacher who moved to an inner-city high school, the coach delivers the Approval Statement stating the teacher really engaged the students and came off as very dynamic, powerful, and interesting when he moved around the room. The coach cites several examples of how his moving around the room improved the delivery of the lesson. Using all the guidelines for an Approval Statement, the coach delivers it in such a way that the teacher is pleased. "Oh, good," he thinks to himself. "I wanted to come across that way in this lesson."

Next the coach notes that despite the fact he or she knows the teacher values the interest he can engage through movement, for a large portion of the lesson the teacher remained at the front of the room in one spot. The coach asks about the teacher's thoughts on arrangement and use of space.

Since the teacher has already received approval for having moved and engaged the students, he knows that he did accomplish that and was capable of doing so again. Because the coach expressed curiosity as to the teacher's thoughts about movement in this lesson, the teacher can respond honestly and together they can explore what occurred and how the teacher might change his behavior in the future. This opens up discussion to move from approval to questions back to approval.

Somewhere within that discussion, the coach can then make his suggestion. It's not like children who receive an extra candle at a birthday party—"one to grow on" at the end of a long list of evaluative phrases. Rather, it works its way out of a conversation in a safe coaching environment; both coach and coachee have the same positive end result in mind. The coach's suggestion in this case outlines a way the teacher can make a note in his written lesson plan to move at certain salient points. To actually put in a symbol on his sheet that indicates "time to move!" "Get interesting, here!" "Keep moving and energizing yourself and your students."

The tone of a postobservation conference changes depending on the teacher's level of experience. A new teacher would need a lot of support and approval with some mild behavioral changes suggested. Someone with more confidence and experience would bring a lot of content information and skill into the room. That teacher would know when he or she was "off" and why, and the coaching would become more in-depth and sophisticated.

THE NEXT PREOBSERVATION CONFERENCE:
A REAL-LIFE EXAMPLE

A good a postobservation conference triggers the next preobservation conference, and the two may occur at the same time. The teacher in our example above asks the coach to watch for his movement in the next observation; to see whether or not the suggestion worked; and to notice how the students reacted, how their level of engagement improved.

Remember our English teachers from Cranford High School? We looked at the preobservation conference between Barbara Carroll and Karen Bailin concerning Karen's complaint that there was too much paperwork and not enough time to be innovative. Karen came up with the idea of having the students create the actual quizzes and topics for discussions, and it was agreed that Barbara would "test-drive" that idea in her Advanced Placement English class.

In chapter 6, we "saw" what happened when Barbara tried out the idea. Karen observed Barbara's lesson plan and noted how the students reacted as they made their presentations and worked in groups.

Karen then decided to try out the lesson plan in her class. Her students are in an "enriched" class, a couple of levels below Barbara's Advanced Placement class. They were reading only one book, *Brave New World*, by Aldous Huxley. She conducted the lesson in a similar format as Barbara, and Barbara observed *her* teaching. They switched roles!

Here's what happened in the postobservation conference immediately following one of the classes:

Barbara: "What thoughts are you having about how it's going?"

Karen: "I don't think it went as well as your class, because I had to keep prompting them for perceptions and insights."

Barbara: "You are disappointed they weren't more insightful."

Karen: "Yes, but I did like that they all participated."

Barbara: "I thought the way you pulled Peter into the group was marvelous."

Karen: "He's always the reluctant one."

Barbara: "You must have inspired him, as he wasn't reluctant today!"

Karen: "Actually, on the days that the students were to present, no one was ever absent. They all showed up to do their part when it was their turn."

Barbara: "You asked me to observe whether or not you were letting the students run the show, stepping back and facilitating. I saw you standing up and leading the group three times; otherwise, they were in charge and you were facilitating their learning."

Karen: "When Rebecca said, 'Lenina's not happy,' that wasn't enough. I could see they weren't using good thinking skills, so I wanted to prompt her for more."

Barbara: "And you did. She thought about it and expressed herself a little more. Actually, the kinds of questions you asked Rebecca and others were similar to coaching questions. You kept them open ended, allowing the students to delve a little deeper."

Karen: "Well, that's true."

Barbara: "I wondered why you did not give the students a choice of books. What made you decide to stick with one book and do the lesson every day?"

Karen: "I didn't know if they were advanced enough or fast enough readers to read three books as in your class."

Barbara: "What other options did you consider?"

Karen: "I thought about having a choice of books. I think if they chose the book, they would like it better and get into it more."

Barbara: "What ways could we structure the lesson so that this was possible?"

So they began restructuring the lesson in order that the students would have a choice of books to read. They agreed that having more choice, a brain-based tool, would empower the students and allow them to take more ownership. They also agreed that the students did very well, considering they were learning a whole new skill set, called teaching!

Looking for new opportunities or options in the postobservation conference segued the same session into a preobservation conference where Karen asked Barbara to help her focus on how and what she wanted Barbara to observe when she launched into this lesson plan again.

The postobservation conference is a place where the most learning can occur between the coach and the coachee. This safe, positive environment allows for positive, clear, and specific feedback, and the benefits of changing behavior if necessary. It is here where the coachee can feel like he or she is advancing as approval is received and feedforward established.

As the coach and teacher review what occurred during the observation, they can then collaborate on solving any problems they noticed or options that present themselves. This, in turn, leads to the next preobservation conference and a new opportunity to experiment, take risks, improve skills, or otherwise advance the profession of teaching.

Sound good? Coaching is extremely effective and supportive of great teaching. It shores up a teacher's self-confidence, provides opportunities for creativity and innovation, and enhances his or her professionalism.

SUMMARY

There's an expression used in film and video production. Whenever a shot isn't right or someone forgets his or her lines, the common phrase is, "That's okay. We'll fix it in post." They are referring to postproduction, where film or video is edited, pasted up, new lines inserted, or problems otherwise ironed out and made perfect.

In a similar way, the postobservation conference allows everything that the teacher and coach have worked on before to come together to be reviewed, patched up, improved upon, and made as perfect as possible for the next performance.

The postobservation conference requires a safe, positive environment, and it requires planning. The coach can use the form suggested or other formats to observe the teacher in a way that leads to the postobservation discussion. Suggestions or ideas for the teacher, along with any questions and, particularly, with comments that focus on what the teacher values—the Approval Statement—are vital for a successful conference.

ANSWERS FOR REPHRASING
NEGATIVE PHRASING TO POSITIVE PHRASING:

1. "Stop using outdated, messy materials."
   Positive Phrasing: "Always use the most professional looking materials."
2. "Don't look only at one side of the room when you are teaching."
   Positive Phrasing: "Look at the whole class when you speak."
3. "Don't slouch when you sit at the conference table."
   Positive Phrasing: "Sit straight at the table, look and feel confident, show an interest."
4. "Stop calling only on boys when you ask a question that involves math."
   Positive Phrasing: "When you ask a question involving math, call on a mix of boys and girls for the answers."
5. "Don't go so fast."
   Positive Phrasing: "Slow down."

The Approval Statement itself requires some skill to deliver. It needs to be based on what the teacher values, what the coach knows has meaning for the coachee, and for that matter, him- or herself. The delivery comes with direct eye contact and a significant pause to both determine if the coachee valued the statement and to allow the approval to sink in.

Invariably, a post-observation conference leads to the next preobservation conference as teacher and coach either want to retry the skill set being observed or add to options by becoming skilled at other techniques.

This cyclical process enhances teaching and student learning along the way. The coach and teacher, in a trusting relationship, also carry that trust and that support to others. In that way, a coaching program within a school or district has the indirect impact of creating a team with high morale, professionalism, and effectiveness.

In chapter 8, we look at ways you can introduce coaching to your school or district.

III

APPLICATIONS OF COACHING

8

I'm Ready! How Do I Create a Coaching Culture?

"**E**very change begins with a conversation," says author, lecturer, and global activist Margaret Wheatley (2002) in *Turning to One Another: Simple Conversations to Restore Hope to the Future.* Likewise, the implementation of every coaching program begins first with a conversation.

I am convinced that coaching programs in schools improve teaching and student learning. They also enhance the professionalism of the staff. Yet I am also aware that each school, district, and organization vastly differs in needs, culture, circumstances, demographics, finances, and personnel. While the coaching process outlined in this book remains the same or is similar in every program, the focus or purpose of the program will differ depending on the circumstances.

Some school districts are experiencing a large influx of beginning teachers who can use direction; others suffer from brain drain, needing new teachers badly. Some schools include vocational and academic tracks and want coaching programs that blend the two. Some schools, in resource-poor communities, suffer from lack of funding; others enjoy grants and funding sources that ensure extras throughout the school.

The rationale for bringing a coaching program into schools with situations such as those described above, or others that may occur, is well rooted in research. Coaching provides the forum for ongoing support on instructional methods, curriculum components, and new formats for instructional delivery. It builds an environment for effective professional development. As we have seen in this book, coaching can move a teacher from good to great. It can create quality in teaching and in learning. Through celebration of achievement and positive feedback, the coaching culture becomes enriched and empowered.

A coachee may share a need with a coach, and the coach's support and feedback helps fill that need. Teaching can be a lonely profession; incorporating a coaching program brings in collaboration, and collaboration inevitably leads to increased resources and options.

Celebrating a teacher's perseverance in conquering a new skill or fine-tuning an already successful lesson plan creates energy for the coach and the coachee. This energy then transfers to students and learning. I encourage all schools that have coaching programs in place to develop celebrations on an ongoing basis for the work that is accomplished. Celebrations give a boost to the ego and make teaching fun. I tell people to keep champagne in the school at all times to celebrate coaching successes. The champagne need not be alcoholic; what people like, and what makes the celebration, is the "pop!"

One of the ways coaching supports people is that it reduces stress. Stress is an everyday fact of life, and in the life of a teacher, stress becomes chronic. We are constantly faced with changes, new technology, new rules, and fast-paced schedules. Stress is ubiquitous, and any support that alleviates its impact creates a more positive environment.

We all know a teacher's role continues to expand. A teacher wears the hats of social worker, guardian, disciplinarian, nutritionist, counselor, psychologist, risk taker, and others too numerous to mention. And did I mention teaching? Teachers deal with minimum competencies, maximum standards; nurturing and nourishing; theory and practice; techniques and strategies; language differences and safety issues. The tasks, like the roles, go on and on.

We looked earlier at quality and Glasser's theory about survival, belonging, power, freedom, and fun. Stress and post-Columbine anxiety has eroded all but the survival stage in many schools. How do we maintain schools that are empowering and enriching, where teaching and learning can be fun?

COACHING ALLEVIATES STRESS

One of the ways a coaching program reduces stress revolves around options. Teachers need as many options as possible to cope, yes, but more importantly to become great teachers. The coach and coachee together collaborate about options, whether in lesson planning or in dealing with stress. Options come from other teachers, videotapes, resources, feedback, shared ideas, and innovations. Coaches and coachees together share resources that assist the coachees in reaching their visions.

Special education teachers know the value of options; they typically use anything they can to reach their students. In fact, many consider using another's resources and ideas as "research!" Why not? The common interest among teachers and students remains to achieve learning. Coaching helps a teacher gain options, and in the process of gaining options, stress can be relieved, if not dissipated. Great teachers are not great because they know what to do. Great teachers are great because they can always think of something *else* to do.

Another important way coaching alleviates stress lies in the trusting relationship a teacher has with his or her coach. The days of a teacher handling everything alone are long gone; there are just too many demands imposed by society, parents, and the very role of teaching. Coaches are in the teacher's corner. They cheer the teacher on, work with teachers to help them succeed. Someone once said having a coach is like having someone's strong, supporting hand held firmly on the back, guiding and also keeping the coachee from falling backward. The kind of guidance and interest coaches provide allows teachers to take a deep breath, relax, and know there is someone there for them.

Ditto for administrators. Those administrators who have undertaken coaching programs report increased energy, enthusiasm for their jobs, reduced stress, a sounder staff, and a district or building with elevated morale. Administrators need coaching too. No one's job has been clearly defined in the past, regardless of degree or experience. Each job has its own distinct and unique features and receives value from coaching.

Confronting Change

I could go on and on about the benefits of coaching, but all those would be moot without a coaching program to back me up. So, how do you begin a coaching program in your school or district? How do you implement something you and the research know is valuable? Well, one way is to begin, as Margaret Wheatley says, with a conversation.

Change can occur in different ways. Often an interested few begin a conversation about changes they would like to see made. Or two people begin e-mailing a third to explore ways they might save time or create situations where they can be more creative. This threesome grows in number, its members talk about what they would like to see occur, and eventually this effects change. Like grassroots causes, the change occurs from the bottom up.

Change from mandate or legislation occurs more rapidly, and it often doesn't garner support as strongly as the groundswell approach. Waiting until a problem or issue becomes so painful that the pain of making change overrides the pain of status quo is another vehicle for change. Finally, change can occur naturally, subconsciously—as an outgrowth of circumstances or shift in perception—and evolve so slowly it is undetected at first. It seems to have suddenly appeared.

Resistance to Change

Before we look at various ways to start a coaching program in a school or district, let's take care of the first event that will occur if the topic is even broached. Beginning a coaching program where none existed represents a change in your school, district, or organization. *Another* one—regardless of method, the overtures of change inevitably meet up with the cymbals of resistance. Bam! Resistance appears to stop coaching programs from forming in schools, just as it does to prevent change from occurring anywhere else.

The most prevalent resistances to coaching are added stress, not enough time, not enough funds, and the perception that coaching really doubles as evaluation. Beyond that, there are ego-related and territorial-related resistances. Resistances you hear in various schools across the country are as follows:

"There is not enough time to do that."

"I'm hesitant to make any more changes."

"I don't need coaching or mentoring; I'm a tenured teacher!"

"My classroom is my terrain; I don't want others in there telling me what to do."

"What if we start it and it doesn't continue? Then what?"

"I'm afraid of another layer of evaluation."

"The whole idea of coaching scares me."

"There's no one to cover my class if I go coach someone else."
"Stress: just one more thing added to my already-full plate."
"Stay out of my classroom!"
"Who does this coach think she or he is?"
"What if I don't measure up?"
"This sounds like another way for the principal to check on me."
"This teacher graduated so long ago, how would she know anything?"
"This is not in my comfort zone."
"I'm not good enough or confident enough to be a coach."

These responses represent real concerns, real fears. They reflect earlier experiences and unpleasant circumstances. Having worked with coaching programs and seen the benefits, however, I know these sources of resistance are easily overcome in most instances. In any case, resistance serves a purpose; rather than being allowed to cause dismay, these responses should be embraced. Without them, change cannot occur. They not only solidify the reasons for change but serve as benchmarks to show that concerns raised by the change were assuaged.

Resistance also slows down the process, serving to ensure that the change benefits the culture and those involved in it. Picture your school, district, or organization as a large bay. Within the bay are boats. Some are speedboats; some are barges. Large rocks jut out from the bottom of the bay, solid reminders from some earlier volcanic eruption.

Speedboats and Barges

Those wanting to immediately introduce a coaching program in the school or district are the speedboats. "Wow. I just read this book by Steve Barkley and we *have* to have coaches in our school *now!*" Six months later, the barges, having heard the cry, finally turned their bows toward the speedboats. "What do we want with coaches? They are velvet things on wheels. Coaches went out with Cinderella!"

"No, no," cry the speedboats. "Coaches are people. We need coaches for teachers! Coaches for administrators! We need a whole coaching program in our school. It will help us. It will improve student learning. It will improve how we do things. We need this *now!*"

The barges carry a lot of the load at schools, districts, or other organizations. They hold the system, the regulations, the rules, the peer pressure, the parents, the curriculum, the administration, the budget, the funding—they weigh a lot! Change will not effectively occur until the barges agree to it. The speedboats, then, need to keep approaching, reminding the barges of the benefits. (Remember the Needs/Benefit Statements from chapter 7? Barges need them too.) Eventually, with sound arguments, meaningful conversation, and a growing number of speedboats, the barges will budge, and the program will be put in place.

The rocks, however, will never budge. They are the holdouts. They will never buy in. They are stuck in the ground, and no amount of wakes washing over them will change that. So the moral of the story is to keep the speedboats from running into the rocks! It's a waste of a speedboat. The speedboats should pool their energy and work on respectfully effecting change with the ones who carry the load—the barges. In time, they will turn around.

MAKING TIME

Coaching programs require time, particularly if they are developed with the trust and rapport to ensure successful coaching relationships. Pre- and postobservation conferences need to be held and time set aside for coaches to observe coachees in classes or in other settings mutually agreed upon. Like the thought of added stress, the thought of something taking more time represents significant resistance when introducing the concept of a coaching program. Time *is* precious. How we use and allocate time concerns not only "getting things done" but also how we nourish and take care of ourselves. Without the latter, the former cannot occur, or not successfully.

Author and entrepreneur Stephen Covey designed an exercise where he puts a clear glass fishbowl on a table in front of a room of people. He then places medium-sized rocks into the bowl until it will hold no more. He asks the group, "Is the bowl full?" Some say yes, some say no.

He then adds smaller rocks—pebbles—that he retrieves from under the table, away from view. He pours the pebbles over the large rocks until the bowl won't hold another pebble. "Is the bowl full now?" Many say yes; a few say no.

Next he pulls out a bag of sand and pours it into the bowl until it reaches the top. Now the response to his question about the fullness of the bowl is a resounding "Yes!"

"Are you sure?" he asks. Some in the group are now skeptical.

Covey then reaches under the table and pulls out a pitcher of water. He pours it into the bowl until it reaches the brim and not another drop can be added.

"Now the bowl is full," says Covey. "And if I had not put the big rocks in first, I would never be able to get them in now." Then he makes his point. What are your "big rocks" in life? If taking care of yourself and your loved ones isn't a big rock, what is? In that way, we can better prioritize time to make it work in ways that serve us.

So how do we introduce the concept and practices of coaching to teachers whose lives already seem filled to the brim? Even if it seems to be a "big rock," an incredibly valuable concept to help in the delivery of sound education, how do we find time to fit it in?

I submit that we do not *find* time; we *make* time! I frequently see educators "give up" on a program because they needed more time to implement it and, after looking for time to do it, can't *find* that time. One teacher lamented that she began a peer coaching strategy with three colleagues (it can start that small, folks), but the program died within two months because they were unable to find common time to observe and confer.

Creativity and risk taking can produce more time. Our existing "boxes" of schedules, classrooms, periods, groups, and job descriptions may be obsolete. In fact, rather than think "out of the box," consider that there *is* no box! What follows are some boxless ways to make time for coaching.

A rural school superintendent wanted enough staff to develop a restructuring effort. There were 250 K–12 students working with twenty-three staff members. The staff determined that five staff members could work with the school's 250 students for one week while the remaining eighteen went to a retreat site to restructure the district. By pairing older and younger students, the five faculty members were able to plan an exciting, educational week for the entire student body. Community volunteers were added for assistance when needed.

Videotape or DVD technology provides another strategy to create time. Videotaping instead of in-class observation increases our flexibility and, therefore, our time. Other faculty members can review a teacher's videotaped lessons for staff development or coaching at free moments. It can even be done at home, at a time more convenient for the coach.

High school science teachers discovered they could provide their students with directions on videotape left with a substitute while the teachers were involved in their coaching sessions. On the tape the teachers modeled the procedures necessary for the assigned work. It increased the substitute's effectiveness, and teachers felt more comfortable leaving their classes to attend the session.

Later these same teachers discovered they could use the videotapes instead of having to give live directions. Students who were absent could watch them. They also began trading tapes with other colleagues. Time lost by making a video created more time for teachers and student growth.

Team teaching is another way to make time. Three teachers can work together on a K–3 team to teach students from four or five classrooms. The teachers who are freed up by this approach can easily participate in their pre- and postobservation coaching conferences.

Finally, here's a strategy for creating a fifteen-hour block of time for school faculty to take part in planning, coaching, or training. Divide the student population by the total number of certified staff in the building. Be sure to include administrators, guidance counselors, specialists, nurses, etc. (My experience shows typically a range of nine to twenty students per staff, with the average being thirteen.)

Have each staff member plan a five-day, two-and-a-half-hour seminar that could be taught to twice the number of students assigned to each staff member, or an average of twenty-six students. In the morning, half of the staff (Staff A) would teach while the second half (Staff B) would have time for planning, staff development, or coaching sessions. They reversed tasks in the afternoon. At the end of one week, students had completed two quality learning experiences while staff gained fifteen hours of time. This was accomplished with no extra cost for substitutes.

This plan works not only on a trial basis for some specific planning or training event but on a more permanent basis. To achieve this, school leaders would need to educate, inform, and share results with school boards and parents to assuage the concerns that time spent outside of direct contact with students might be considered wasted. If the time is spent in coaching and planning, that's hardly the case.

COACHING IS NOT EVALUATING

The importance of basing a coach-coachee relationship on trust is paramount. Remember that evaluators work for the system; coaches work for the coachee. Coaching is entirely nonevaluative and is based on what the coachee has requested that he or she wants to improve. The content of comments, observations, or feedback made to the coachee is solely between the coach and coachee.

Checking in and reframing the relationship as it evolves often occurs at the beginning of a coaching program. We are all so ingrained with the mentality of judging that coaching seems almost too good to be true. The coach is there to work with you on whatever *you* want, not what he or she wants. That represents a completely different shift in perception and behavior from an evaluative relationship.

Trust means saying what you're going to do and then doing it. Saying you're going to coach and then offering unsolicited advice, opinion, or judgment flies in the face of the trust established in the relationship. To ensure that this context of coaching remains separate from evaluating, it's very useful to establish norms and guidelines about the coaching relationship, as mentioned in chapter 5.

Norms are established with full participation of all involved in the coaching program. I recommend that they be written and, where possible, posted. As others join the program, they buy into the norms or agreement and may even suggest new ones, which all are then asked to agree to. Mutual agreement not only solidifies the concept of coaching being separate from evaluating but serves as a guidepost. When someone leans toward evaluation, one needs simply point to the norm and say, "We have agreed not to do that in this program."

IDENTIFYING THE PROBLEMS COACHING CAN RESOLVE

Dealing with the issues of stress, time, and the fear that coaching may be like evaluation paves the way for beginning and implementing a successful coaching program. Another approach consists of highlighting the issues or circumstances that point to the need for a coaching program. Identifying the problems that exist and gaining agreement on what those problems are lead to a discussion of how coaching can solve the problem. There are a couple of ways to do this, both of which open the conversation that leads to the development of a coaching program.

Susan Scott's *Fierce Conversations* provides a technique of probing for what she calls "mineral rights"—the underlying issue or issues—through asking probing questions. The probe goes to an individual as well as to a group, and the process uncovers an issue and its impact, while also paving the way for creating action plans to resolve it. Using the probing technique to advance the cause of a coaching program not only highlights the need for the program but solidifies how people are feeling and how they are impacted in the school generally. Here's what the probing questions might sound like:

Step 1: Identify the most pressing issue. "The issue that we most need to resolve is . . ."

Step 2: Clarify the issue. "What's going on?" "How long has it been going on?" "How bad are things?"

Step 3: Determine current impact. "How is this issue currently impacting me?" "What results are currently being produced by this situation?" "How is this issue currently impacting others?" "What results are currently being produced for them by this situation?" "When I consider the impact on myself and others, what are my feelings or emotions?"

Step 4: Uncover future implications. "If nothing changes, what's likely to happen?" "What's at stake for me relative to this issue?" "What's at stake for others?" "When I consider these possible outcomes, what are my emotions."

Step 5: Examine personal contributions to this issue. "What is *my* contribution to this issue?" ("How have I contributed to the problem?")

Step 6: Describe the ideal outcome. "When this issue is resolved, what difference will that make?" "What results will I enjoy?" "When this issue is resolved, what results will others enjoy?" "When I imagine this resolution, what are my emotions?"

Step 7: Commit to action. "What is the most potent step I could take to move this issue toward resolution?" "What's going to attempt to get in my way and how will I get past it?" "When will I take this step?"

Contract with myself: Here Scott suggests that you identify what you are willing to do to move things along, that your contract is with yourself.

Contract with others: What others have indicated they are willing to do to move the program along or to work toward resolving the issue.

After all this probing and soul searching, Scott suggests, "Take a break. Walk around. Breathe. Breathing is good."

Using a Force-Field Analysis

Another way problems can be identified and thus lead to the goal of implementing a coaching program relies on employing a simple instrument called a Force Field Analysis developed by Kurt Lewin, shown on page 164, figure 8.1.

An identified problem—possibly uncovered through probing questions—is written in the top box. This reflects the current state of affairs, Current Situation. Desired Change, the second box, represents a goal, such as a school-wide coaching program.

In the example on page 165, figure 8.2, we have identified a problem for Current Situation as "not enough time or money for needed, off-site staff development training for teachers." That is summarized as "Not enough teacher training."

The Desired Change is "to bring in a consultant to develop an 'in-house' training on coaching that provides the opportunity for the school or district to carry on with the coaching program without having to resort to frequent off-site staff development." So the goal is succinctly stated as "Implement in-house coaching program."

The left column below the two boxes lists "Forces for Change." These represent driving forces that would move toward the goal. These forces encourage change to occur. The forces may include available resources, readiness and desire of staff, flexibility of schedules, agreement between administration and staff, support by parents, availability of grant funding, and the research we explored earlier that points to improvements in teaching and learning when a coaching program is in place.

The "Forces against Change" column lists obstacles or restraining forces that may prevent change from happening. All the factors that may impede the desired change should be listed here and broken down into individual elements if they look too broad based. These forces may consist of insufficient staff to cover teachers doing coaching, staff resistance to coaching, time and schedule restraints, lack of funding, lack of interest by the administration, lack of available rooms to conduct conferences, etc.

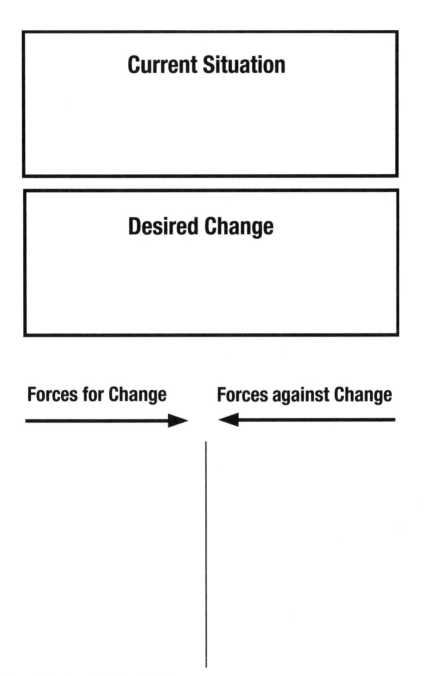

Figure 8.1. Force Field Analysis Form

Current Situation

Not enough
teacher training.

Desired Change

Implement in-house
coaching program.

Forces for Change   **Forces against Change**

Forces for Change	Forces against Change
Available resources	Insufficient staff to cover
Readiness & desire of staff	Staff resistance
Flexible schedules in place	Not enough time
Staff/admin agreement	Lack of funding
Parent support	Administration not interested
Grant money available	Lack of meeting spaces
Teacher/student improvement	

Figure 8.2.   Force Field Analysis Implementing Coaching

Next, you rank the Forces against Change according to those that are strongest and thus most difficult to change as shown in figure 8.3, page 167. You do the same prioritization with the Forces for Change as to their strengths.

A little hint here: The benefits of coaching can be included on the Forces for Change side. Each Force against Change can be offset by a Force for Change. For example, the Force against Change may be lack of time. As we know from considering ways to "make time," the strongest Force for Change may be a willingness to be flexible in scheduling.

As you identify and prioritize the forces for and against the change, a solution often appears. In the example in figure 8.3, there is readiness among the staff and flexible schedules are already in place, yet there is a lack of interest by the administration and insufficient funds. Those were identified as the strongest forces on either side, for and against the Desired Change (indicated by the bold face lines and check marks in figure 8.3).

What this reveals, however, is the possibility that the readiness and desire by staff might be capitalized upon to convince the administration of the value of the program. There is also parent support and grant money available that might help generate the funding needed to carry out the program.

Each Force Field Analysis will tell its own tale, and the process serves as a useful model to identify the real factors involved in making a positive change. Since all coaching programs are customized to the circumstances of the school or district, this model can also help identify the kind of program that might work for you. If the Forces against Change outnumber the Forces for Change, rather than scrap the idea of a coaching program, reframe its format to fit your situation. Then you fill out this model again and see if the Forces against Change diminish.

INTRODUCING COACHING

Armed with tools to counteract resistance to a coaching program, there remains the step of introducing it. This can be one conversation between two teachers willing to help one another. It might evolve to a group of teachers meeting to create a program. The principal may wish to start a coaching program, or the teachers may present the administrator with an outline of the program they desire and why.

Current Situation

Not enough
teacher training.

Desired Change

Implement in-house
coaching program.

Forces for Change

→

Available resources

✔ **Readiness & desire of staff**

✔ **Flexible schedules in place**

Staff/admin agreement

Parent support

Grant money available

Teacher/student
improvement

Forces against Change

←

Insufficient staff to cover

Staff resistance

Not enough time

✔ **Lack of funding**

✔ **Administration not interested**

Lack of meeting spaces

Figure 8.3.   Force Field Analysis Coaching Solution

In schools with more experienced staff, coaching may be implemented as an alternative to evaluation. If most teachers have skill levels above the system's minimum competence covered in traditional evaluations, they could transfer to a coaching program.

In my experience as a trainer, a coaching program usually gets under way correctly with peer coaching training.

TWO SCHOOLS

Improving school for students is the practical reason for incorporating coaching, and therefore empowerment, into a teaching environment. Let's look at how students receive ultimate benefit from having a coaching program in place.

In a school where one teacher is responsible for a set number of students with no possibility for help from others—a situation we'll call School No. 1—coaching takes a back burner if it exists at all, as there is no help available. This represents the standard school of the past, where the teacher is isolated in his or her classroom. The teacher welcomes a group of students to his or her classroom at the beginning of the school year. This teacher teaches these individuals throughout the year until they leave in the spring, to come back in the fall to a different grade. The teacher then welcomes a new group of individuals, and the cycle begins again.

In School No.1, teachers have no responsibility to assist other colleagues; they are in charge only of their individual students. If a teacher has a problem with low-performing students, there is no help. Low performers get ignored, transferred, or put into a negative category that will mark them for the rest of their school life, if not their whole lives. If the teacher does not know how to keep a high-performing student engaged, there are no suggestions from other teachers, no options.

School No. 2 does things differently. Rather than follow the model of individual teachers responsible for a group of individual students with no possibility for support, in School No. 2 every student belongs to every teacher. Each teacher is responsible for the success of every classroom. Teachers work not as individuals but as a team. Students who are having trouble get the full support of the teaching *team*, and they feel it. In School No. 1, teachers and students are isolated. Here teachers are part of a team that works together to ensure the success of all students.

In reality, individual teachers can no longer take a group of kids into a classroom and be successful by themselves. They must have an intimate involvement with teachers that students had the previous year, the ones they will be having the following year, and anyone else involved with them, from other teachers to parents to sports coaches, etc.

One option in a school that affirms everyone's responsibility for all students is to create a vertical team. For example, the team consists of first-, second-, and third-grade teachers in an elementary school. Let's say a beginning teacher teaches second grade. The scaffolding for the teamwork is coaching. Let's say the second-grade teacher has every student who was previously in the first-grade class. It's only natural for the first- and second-grade teachers to collaborate and for the first-grade teacher to assist the beginning second-grade teacher—ditto for the second- and third-grade teachers. Every student will pass through each of their classrooms, so it is in their best interest to help one another. Teachers benefit from the knowledge and support of the others, and three guesses who benefits the most—the students.

Sometimes there is a crossover from School No. 1 and School No. 2. A staff of teachers—the teaching team—may focus on a whole group of students, such as sixth-grade teachers focusing on all sixth-grade students. Or it may go the other way—an individual teacher may take care of individual students.

For the most part, however, the model of School No. 2—with a teaching team responsible for all students—benefits from coaching, and it benefits from the synergy that occurs when a team of focused educators takes every student into account. You will know when your school is moving to the School No. 2 model by the number of times individual student names appear on the agenda of your staff meetings. The more often the agenda lists names of students who may need help or input from all on the teaching team rather than simply curriculum or system issues, the more it is evident that your school is focused on individual students and the closer you are to arriving at School No. 2 status.

Large-School Solutions

Is your school too big to have every teacher responsible for every student? Here's an example of how the model similar to many advisor/advisee programs can be implemented in a large high school. Take the number of students in the high school and divide that number by the number of faculty. Each faculty member takes responsibility for a team of kids, often only sixteen students. That teacher—we'll call him Al—would attend parent conferences for each of the students on his team. Al would be the guy the student goes to for guidance, assistance, and support. Let's say Al teaches English and that a student is having a whole lot of trouble in chemistry. In the model of coaching and collaboration, Al simply consults the student's chemistry teacher, and together they work on a plan to help the student.

This model can work in reverse as well. The chemistry teacher has 120 students, and there is no way he or she can know every one of them. If there are a couple of kids acting up in chemistry class, usually at the instigation of one student named Vince, the chemistry teacher goes to Al, who is the advisor for Vince, and they consult.

What we're really talking about creating are small learning communities within a large school. Those teachers responsible for a set number of students have their own communities of students. Unlike having these individuals in a classroom, however, the advisor gets to know them in all aspects of their learning. The advisors—the "Als"—always have access to the other teachers who teach or otherwise work with the students.

Small Learning Communities

Today many schools look at creating small learning communities, in order to increase the focus on individual student success. Some middle schools form sixth-, seventh-, and eighth-grade "houses" where teams of teachers have three-year responsibility for these students. Teachers coaching colleagues within these houses greatly increases the sense of collaboration and at the same time provides a model of cooperation for students.

Let's say one house of advisors consists of math teachers from each grade. They would help students as they travel from sixth to eighth grade, minimizing repetition of content. This system allows the student to build on his math skills from year to year with a common and familiar language, and it gives students the full support of their teachers throughout their middle school years.

In my estimation, School No. 1 is obsolete, although sadly many schools still operate in that model. To move from School No. 1 to the model of School No. 2, coaching is vital. Coaching creates the teamwork necessary to serve students. The trust associated with coaching allows teachers to "let go" of their individual classrooms, seek options, gain support from others, and share in failures and successes. By "let go," I mean share in the wealth of ideas generated in the classroom. The teacher needs no longer be possessive and protective of the students; they belong to all the teachers.

Opportunities for celebrations are embedded in coaching and collaboration among teachers who are focused on the success of every student. As an individual teacher succeeds in getting a student to read or stop acting up or to engage in a lesson, the whole team can celebrate the success of that student as "our" student.

SUMMARY

Over the years, I have seen countless ways coaching has benefited the profession of educators, whether teachers, administrators, principals, or staff members. More importantly, students benefit from teachers who are confident, effective, highly skilled, and yes, *happy* because they have coaches to rely on for support and encouragement.

Adding coaching increases quality in a school environment. Teachers and students alike can move beyond the survival mode and well into the freedom and fun of learning, collaborating, and creating together. Teachers can move from good to great. Time can be freed up through creative solutions that not only allow for the structure of the coaching process but bring much-needed time to reflect and innovate.

Following the process of a preobservation conference, where the teachers' vision and agenda are uncovered, observing, and then giving feedback in the postobservation conference becomes natural and smooth with time. Eventually, those being coached are unable to conceive of teaching without the benefit of coaching. The coachee is the focus, yet the coach also learns, improves, and is rewarded by the successes of his or her protégé. What's not to like?

To implement a coaching program, one needs to identify the issue and the goal and then just begin. All change begins with a conversation. There are lots of ways to format a coaching program and many applications for it.

In chapter 9, you will see case studies and examples of coaching programs under way throughout the United States. If you are not already inspired to benefit from the significantly positive impact that coaching can have on your school, district, or organization, perhaps you'll find additional motivation in these actual success stories.

9

Who Has Coaching Programs?
How Are They Working?

Earlier we pointed out that coaching programs and coaching relationships vary from person to person and from school to school. In this chapter you will find a half-dozen examples of coaching programs around the country that are working. Each tells its own story. Some may motivate you to begin now to implement a coaching program of your own at your school or district. You have all the skills, tools, knowledge, and, I hope, motivation to succeed.

Good luck!

COLLEGIAL COACHING GROUP

One could say teachers were among the first entrepreneurs. We all have the image of the schoolteacher moving out west, opening a one-room schoolhouse and teaching all the kids in town. Today teachers enter a classroom, close the door behind them, and teach primarily on their own. They rely on their years of education and experience, and they do the best they can.

Sometimes, though, it's nice to have a little help from your friends.

At Winter Park Tech in Orange County, Florida, teachers and administrators decided to circle the wagons and work together to improve everyone's professional abilities. Winter Park has an academic track and an occupational track. A need was perceived to build stronger connections between the teaching staffs and administrators in the school.

Several faculty members participated in a training program of coaching skills by Performance Learning Systems (PLS), a national provider of staff development training for educators and administrators. Participants developed skills to improve rapport among colleagues, resulting in positive instructional change and enhanced self-esteem. Eventually all faculty—teachers and administrators alike—took the PLS coaching program.

An idea born of those staff-development sessions took the coaching concepts learned and encouraged further support among faculty in a more informal setting. Thus was formed a "collegial coaching group." The response was tremendous. Twenty of forty-five faculty members showed up at the initial meeting and immediately wanted to continue the process started in staff development, meeting every other week.

"The coaching process opens communication," says Judy Sheehan, curriculum resource director at Winter Tech and facilitator of the collegial coaching sessions. "We really *talk* to one another using the coaching concepts we learned. We're not just broad-brushing our feedback by saying, 'Oh, you did fine' or 'That was nice.' It's specific, and the focus is always on the one being coached," she adds.

Thirty-minute after-school sessions cover topics such as classroom management, communication, presentation skills, team-building activities, use of peer evaluations, and student motivation techniques. Summaries of each session are e-mailed to all faculty members.

"The benefit of the collegial coaching group is that teachers and administrators share ideas, brainstorm solutions to common teaching challenges, and learn from one another," says Winter Park director Diane Culpepper. "Where they didn't mingle before, now they are mixing together, visiting each other's classrooms."

"Faculty support has been pleasantly surprising," says Sheehan. "There has been a lot of attendance by highly experienced teachers willing to share with more beginning teachers. The meetings have almost taken on the dynamics of group therapy sessions," she laughs. "We sit in a circle and share our ideas and experiences in a nonthreatening atmosphere. This coaching program has been a great boon to our school."

JOB-EMBEDDED PROFESSIONAL DEVELOPMENT

"I want to know if I'm dominating the meeting, if I'm pushing too hard," said Judy Hennessey, superintendent of Oakwood City School District in Ohio.

"What behaviors would you say are 'dominating'?" responded Debbie Smith, a computer science and journalism teacher at Oakwood City High School.

A conversation such as this occurred between the superintendent and teacher in a preconference coaching session where Debbie was coaching her "boss." Judy was about to attend an important meeting and was outlining behaviors on which she felt she needed coaching. (You may recall this conversation from earlier in the book.)

In turn, Judy coached Debbie at a future session where Debbie specifically wanted to know how quickly she was able to engage her students in the classroom. These are samples of many such conversations held districtwide among teachers, administrators, the director of curriculum, and the superintendent in this district of 1,900 students, four buildings, and 150 staff members.

The conversations occurred as a result of staff-development training in the skills of peer coaching that began in August 2001 with fifty staff members, including all nine administrators. It has since grown to encompass nearly a third of the school population, with plans to continue the coaching program until all teachers and administrators have been trained.

"Our district's philosophy is to include job-embedded professional development wherever possible," says Dr. Mary Jo Scalzo, director of curriculum, instruction, and assessment. "We believe the job-embedded aspect critical because teachers are working with one another on technical practice in the classroom. With peer coaching, there's someone *there* for them. The process always focuses on the one being coached," she adds.

Initially, the district brought in a training consultant, who spent three days with the fifty participants teaching and practicing peer coaching skills. These included specific questioning skills, listening skills, and a process that allowed practice and continuation of learning from the training, adding to skills that could be used in the classroom or the boardroom.

"The consultant has remained very accessible to us," says Hennessey. "He comes back frequently and is also available to coach us by phone. He really wants us to be empowered with this and doesn't want us to need him to come back! That's very compelling in a consultant."

The process used consists of a preconference meeting between the coach and the coachee. The coach interviews the coachee using specific questioning skills. The purpose of the interview is to determine specifically what the coachee believes, what he or she wants the coach to focus on during the observation phase, and the data he or she wants collected by the coach.

This preobservation conference is followed by the actual observation, where one teacher or one administrator attends the class and provides the data and feedback requested of the coachee—and nothing else. The postobservation conference consists of a debriefing and feedback of what went on, how the coachee measured up to his or her own criteria.

"The coaching process opens communication, raises it to a higher level of technical discussion," observes Hennessey. "Those trained are not going to engage in global statements such as 'good job,' or 'nice.' We're very careful to draw it back to what the person has asked for."

To pay for this ongoing staff development training in the art and skill of coaching—as well as other professional education—teachers literally pooled their resources. In their 2000–2001 master agreement, they negotiated for the development of a Professional Development Committee (PDC) consisting of six teachers and two administrators. The major responsibility of the PDC is to authorize funding requests by teachers for professional staff development training. Prior to that time, each building was given funds to appropriate for training among the staff in that building. An allotment of $175 was equally provided to each teacher each year. A teacher could use it or save it over the life of the contract to put toward a more expensive endeavor. Most attended conferences.

Once the PDC was formed, the allotments were abandoned, and all the money was pooled into one central account to be administered by the PDC—a total of approximately $103,000 each year. Teachers requested the necessary amount for the training they wanted to receive. While the principal had to approve each training activity, the PDC decided on the level of funding. Priority was given to teams of teachers who attend a conference together as well as collaborative endeavors, such as book study groups, action research, or, in the case of the peer coaching program, the hiring of a consultant to provide training.

According to Scalzo, teachers have become more aware of the type of professional staff development they need and can benefit from as a result of coaching. Over a two-year period, the PDC funded the high school math department with investment in an Integrated Mathematics Program. The PDC provided funds for weeklong seminars, secured on-site consultants, paid for attendance at national and state conferences, and even provided dinners for after-school department meetings.

"Teachers could never have accomplished this on their allotment of $175," says Scalzo. "And, we could not have brought in a consultant to train us as peer coaches without this funding model. As a result, we've 'grown' sixty peer coaches, which includes twenty to twenty-five teachers new to the district. And we're going to continue to grow them," she adds.

Beyond hiring a consultant, the teachers and administrators who serve as peer coaches to each other do follow-up practice on their own. They become in-house experts and gain skills as they practice.

One coaching team videotaped its preconference session and shared it with other trained coaches. The team conducted its postconference session "live" in front of the group, receiving feedback on the feedback.

The impact of the coaching program on teaching shows up in the interaction among teachers to improve their skills in a nonjudgmental environment that provides reinforcement as well as feedback. This in turn has had an effect on student learning.

"I have seen that it really causes teachers to critically examine why they're doing what they're doing and to focus on learner activities," says Oakwood City High School principal Joe Boyle. "They begin to focus more clearly on how they're doing as a result of recently being coached. The reflection is about how well they make their presentations to the learner."

Boyle was himself coached by enrichment teacher Amanda Ammer, one of the team of peer coaches who put together the videotaped conference, and vice versa. "Because of my experience with coaching," says Ammer, "I have become more aware of my questioning skills. As coach, Joe helped me evaluate the types of questions I was asking my students. I wanted to gather information on my questioning skills because I want to ask higher level questions that elicit critical thinking."

Debbie Smith, the teacher who coached Superintendent Hennessey, recalls that during her coaching session at a closed session with the district's board of trustees, she gained a new insight into the superintendent's role and how she works with the community to get what the district needs.

"One of the spin-offs of this training is that it gives me a support group," says Melissa Gambill, an English teacher of twenty-five years' experience. "Beyond the actual coaching sessions, I find we are talking more about mutual concerns, like 'are we overdoing the time we spend grading term papers?' There is a level of respect for each other's opinions, and we can share in our goal of being better teachers."

In essence, the coaching program works because of a willingness and dedication to make it work. Time is an issue—or, as Scalzo quips, "the tyranny of the urgent interferes with what we're all about as educators." It became important to continue to motivate the teachers to attend coaching sessions. They even scheduled a two-day off-site retreat for those involved in the program to reinforce the benefits they were receiving.

"It's not from lack of will or interest that they find themselves squeezing training into their day. It's just that everything else vies for their time as well," said Scalzo.

The consultant provided several days of intermittent training, but the internalization of that training really occurred as teachers and administrators worked together to practice and implement what they learned. This not only maximized their staff development monies but empowered the whole team of educators to support one another to improve student learning.

"I am just so encouraged that teachers at all levels of skill are finding common ground, having technical discussions—Joyce and Showers type discussions," says Hennessey. "And these discussions are focused on what they do as teachers—the heart of what we are trying to accomplish as human beings and as teachers. And it's all in a nonthreatening environment. We can celebrate the fact that people are willing to look at their teaching in specific ways—really get into how they are effective and successful. And ultimately we may not need a consultant at all!"

COACHING FOR TEACHERS OF STRUGGLING READERS

In their quest for ways to improve the achievement of struggling readers, the school district of Hillsborough County, in Tampa, Florida, the tenth-largest school district in the United States, began a K–3 Reading Coaches project in 1999–2000. While this teacher-coaching project focuses on reading instruction, teaching strategies and management issues are important components.

"We build in lots of opportunities to mentor one another," says Cheryl Jones, supervisor of the Reading First Grant in the district's Elementary Education Department. "We set aside time at our regular bimonthly meetings for coaches to interact with each other for support, problem solving, and sharing of successes."

Coaching applicants recruited through districtwide advertisements undergo a rigorous screening process that includes an interview designed to assess their level of content knowledge and interpersonal skills. The interview is often followed by classroom observations and discussions with the applicant's principal. Applicants who pass this screening process are accepted into the training program.

Their training begins during the school year with bimonthly meetings. Coaches receive assignments that help them implement the techniques and strategies learned in training. District personnel, members of the elementary language-arts team, conduct classroom observations of the reading coaches during this process in order to better understand each coach's strengths and weaknesses. They use this information to help customize the training to better meet their needs.

A mandatory summer institute conducted in June follows the year of training. It includes a program (at several school sites) that accommodates the Reading Coach practicum. For the practicum, coaches work in pairs each morning to deliver classroom instruction that reflects their training and allows them to practice their coaching skills by coaching their partners. Each afternoon they attend additional training. Then they conduct exit interviews at the close of this institute to summarize each coach's progress, debrief their learning, target areas for continued growth, and receive feedback about the effectiveness of the training program.

"I believe the outstanding quality of our program stems from the strenuous selection process and training that each coach must successfully complete before becoming a Reading Coach," says Jones. "We continue our model of professional growth with two training sessions each month."

The K–3 Reading Coach program in Hillsborough County includes sixty-two coaches working at 108 schools. To date, nearly 2,500 teachers throughout the district have worked with the reading coaches. Schools also use Reading Coaches as a conduit whereby information, teaching techniques, and reading process studies can be disseminated efficiently and effectively to teachers. The coaching program has also provided a strong cadre of trainers to deliver districtwide training in reading.

In the first year of the project, the district trained coaches in schools with the highest levels of poverty and the lowest test scores in reading. At the end of that first year, Dr. Grace Albritton of the Department of Accountability, Assessment, and Evaluation conducted a study to evaluate the Reading Coach Project. The impact was immediate and clear: Students at these schools performed at the national average or above. The study is ongoing and continues to provide encouraging data.

As might be predicted, some resistance to the project occurred in the initial stages at the teacher, school site administrator, and district levels. Resistance from the district level came about because the project pulled some of the best teachers from the classroom just as the district was facing a teacher shortage. The expense of the initiative was an additional concern.

In addition, some administrators had difficulty understanding the role and purpose of the coach. They struggled with the idea that the program did not use coaches to pull small groups of struggling readers but rather worked one on one with their teachers. Program coordinators worked with the administrators to protect the trust inherent in the individual coaching process and assisted them in understanding that coaches were not in an evaluative role, nor were they to be enlisted as substitutes or for administrative duties.

Top-level administrative resistance was diminished by the strong research base that supported the coaching program. The resistance was further reduced when the results of Dr. Albritton's study showed a profound impact by improving reading skills and teacher morale.

School administrators' issues were dealt with through written information that clearly defined the roles and responsibilities of the coach. In addition, principals and assistant principals participated in staff development that focused on coaching and helped them better understand the purpose of the project.

"Teachers continue to provide the greatest level of resistance," adds Jones. "Some have a difficult time accepting the fact that the coach is there to support them, not evaluate them. Some also resist the changes brought about by working with a coach."

Teacher resistance diffused as the coaches implemented their coaching skills to uncover teachers' agendas and concerns and to provide support and feedback in an environment of trust. Program coordinators also worked with administrators to demonstrate the value of coaching, garner support, and enlist their help in encouraging teachers to work with their coach.

"We find it takes time to build trust," concludes Jones. "We have to be vigilant and keep our coaches encouraged as they work through the initial stages of teacher resistance. Once that happens, we find that it is well worth the effort."

COACHING AND LEARNING-STYLES TRAINING

At Hillsborough County School District the small beginnings of a coaching and learning styles training resulted in the development of a full-fledged online program that combines coaching and learning styles. Now the districtwide adopted slogan says, "If you build it, they will come!"

A live training in coaching skills for administrators, mentors, reading coaches, and National Board Certified teachers beginning in 2000 resulted in a collaborative and integrated online program being made available to thirteen thousand teachers and instructional personnel in 190 schools throughout the school district. Those previously trained as coaches and mentors work at individual school sites to assist teachers as they implement the coaching and learning styles programs obtained in both an online format and in a face-to-face, blended form of learning.

"We offered an online learning program to our clerical and administrative staff as a pilot program," says Jodi Lamb, supervisor of staff development. "It was quite successful, and we began to get calls from mentors at several school sites asking for online training."

By 2001, the online coaching and learning styles course had been made available to the entire district. Those who have already taken the live coaching training have online access to the online coaching/learning-styles course as a refresher. The combination of coaching and learning styles serves not only to enhance the teaching strategies of educators but to build collaboration among professionals throughout the district.

According to Lamb, an issue at Hillsborough that is shared by many other school districts across the nation is the need to train beginning teachers. An urban school district, Hillsborough recruits 1,200 new teachers a year. Beyond that, the district's enrollment increases by five thousand students a year, creating a tremendous need for staff-development training of beginning teachers. Reaching out to all of these new teachers on a continuous basis with appropriate follow-up and feedback can be difficult. The online program at Hillsborough promises to cut through these barriers and provide multiple and alternative ways to support the teacher's learning.

For a new teacher, receiving coaching and assistance on the concepts and strategies of learning styles can provide a substantial boost to lesson planning, teaching options, and communication with students. It allows teachers to identify and work with their *own* learning styles and then work to rotate that style to reach all learners. The coaching component, both online and on-site, builds their confidence and fine-tunes their approach to teaching.

The blended live and online training model in coaching and in learning styles provided by Hillsborough County School District underscores a commitment to provide a combination to continue to attract professionals committed to excellence in teaching. They keep building it, and people keep coming.

COACHING "SUCCESSFUL" TEACHERS

Cranford Public Schools in Cranford, New Jersey, started its coaching program in the fall of 2003. Its focus was on coaching teachers already experiencing success rather than those needing remediation. Coaches were invited to participate and were paired with teachers. Approximately forty people participated in the program.

Sessions, initially held with an educational consultant from Performance Learning Systems, included the district administrator, principals, and supervisors, who were paired with teachers in coaching relationships. Since communication skills were a large part of the training, coaches were also paired, to practice them with one another.

Joseph Corriero, Ed.D., Assistant Superintendent for Curriculum and Instruction, serves on the Cranford Board of Education. Corriero worked with a third-grade teacher who had coached him in the preliminary stages. "That gave me a completely different perspective," says Corriero. "Our relationship expanded from that experience." In a reversed role, his coach, Tracy Mastice, was having difficulty in a noncoaching relationship with a student teacher. She felt comfortable talking to Corriero about it. "Rather than looking at it from an administrative or bureaucratic point of view," says Corriero, "I looked at it from a personal view. This completely shifted how I approached the situation. Tracy also wanted me to coach her on teaching math to her third graders, and I was pleased to help her with that as well. She even allowed me to videotape her for use in the training programs," he adds.

This district sees coaching as a powerful form of staff development. Teachers have the opportunity to forgo traditional evaluation procedures and undertake other unique processes, such as coaching. Coaching is used as a professional development plan and it suffices for evaluation.

Barbara Carroll and Karen Bailin, the two English teachers who coached one another as documented in other chapters of this book, remain members of the Cranford coaching program.

FIVE-YEAR-OLD COACHING PROGRAM

In chapter 1, I reported that when Stillwater, Oklahoma, teacher Cindy Petree went to a coaching session offered by PLS, she took a deep breath, swallowed, and admitted to other teachers that she wished she was as good a teacher working on her own as she was when she knew someone was watching her. To her surprise, others often felt exactly the same way. Cindy knew then that peer coaching was about to become a big part of her life.

That was five years ago. Petree now participates with fifteen teachers in a training of trainers coaching program developed by PLS. These teacher-trainers now educate 120 to 150 teachers and administrators annually.

"The coaching program started under a Professional Development Institute (PDI) grant," says Leah Engelhardt, a College of Education professor at Oklahoma State University. "It initially aimed at beginning teachers to offset an attrition rate of about 13 percent. PLS consultant

Miriam Georg was brought in to teach our first forty-five-hour graduate coaching course. What has happened since then is a blossoming of participation in this coaching program to encompass the entire state."

Engelhardt points out that the state initially thought teachers participating in the coaching course could begin teaching others right away. "Well, that was just not so," she emphasizes. "There's a lot more to this than meets the eye."

In Petree's case, she took the coaching course and then opted to return to learn more about how she could eventually teach it to others. In Year Two, she learned to facilitate under the guidance of PLS. In Year Three, teachers taught some modules themselves. By Year Four, the consultant was coming only briefly and the trainers were teaching by themselves. By Year Five, they were completely on their own.

Those coached in this program received a 95 percent retention rating, according to a report issued by the PDI. While the consultant continued to draw away from the program, empowering teachers to carry on without her, the interest and retention of teachers increased.

"I really believe in this program," says Petree. "When we first began, we related to one another as teaching colleagues, but we didn't really share any techniques or skills about teaching. We never discussed our challenges. I guess we were afraid we might not look good.

"Now we're actually *training* one another," she laughs. "The program has gained an excellent reputation in the state. People come by choice— all ages, all subjects, all levels, all experiences. Yet I still see apprehension about having teaching practices scrutinized. As we go along, the barriers fall. I see people opening up, sharing their challenges, tips, and techniques—helping one another grow. There's lots of trust—it's wonderful!"

As to how it has impacted her teaching, Petree says she has become more proactive in coaching herself and more reflective of her own teaching.

Is this type of program replicable? "Just build it, and they will come!" says Engelhardt. "This program developed teachers into good presenters, good coaches, and definitely better teachers. It really works."

COLLABORATIVE COACHING PROGRAMS

The goal at fast-growing Orange County Public Schools in Orlando, Florida, is to develop collaborative schools. The Leadership Development

Center there encompasses a variety of programs geared toward modeling collaboration among teachers, administrators, and staff in ways that then translate to improved student learning.

The Orange County collaborative attended training on coaching with the National Educator Program, a collaboration of the National Education Association (NEA), Stetson University, and Performance Learning Systems. The live on-site training took place at Stetson's satellite campus in Disney's Celebration City, where fifteen administrators from selected schools within the district learned the value and techniques of coaching. Two teachers from each school accompanied them.

Now administrators are working with educators in a customized staff development training that blends coaching skills with learning styles instruction. The program combines on-site training with online learning and calls for periodic meetings and feedback sessions among the learner-participants. In-depth on-site sessions delivered by PLS in leadership, instructional coaching, and learning styles at the fifteen school sites rounded out the program.

Of paramount importance in the program is the inclusion of administrators and educators in the learning process. "Professional development has to have leadership advocacy to work," says Dr. Nora Gledich, director of Orange County Florida's Leadership Development Council). "It is a requirement that every principal from these selected schools be involved in the learning program."

The focus of the training is thus another collaboration—that of two professionals seeking to understand educational strategies that lead to higher standards of teaching and learning. The computer-based learner benefits when applying the skills learned online in a classroom setting. He or she has the collaboration of a person trained both in the online learning styles program and in "live" training of coaching skills geared to help teachers improve their knowledge and use of learning styles in the classroom, analyze daily practices, and make instructional changes accordingly. It is clear from this program that Orange County models the collaborative goals it hopes to achieve in all their schools.

Another form of "collaboration" is the collaborative effect of various teaching methods. In addition to the knowledge presented, the essential components of live interaction, feedback, coaching, and practice are included in staff-development training. "To simply put written materials online is not responsible training," says a PLS spokesperson. "And to achieve the components of training that research and experience show work best there needs to be in place a combination of high quality technical expertise, willing educational organizations, innovative sponsoring universities, and administrative and educator personnel eager to learn in this new medium."

The partnership of training experts and educators in the Orange County model provides these essential components. Most importantly, it addresses the vital need to monitor and account for the learning that takes place. "Someone needs to give an overview to the teacher-users," adds Gledich. "There needs to be coordination, monitoring, and probably most important, motivation to continue the learning program online. In short, relationship needs to accompany the drone of the computer screen," she adds.

SUMMARY

Highly successful coaching programs are embedded in schools around the country. By every account, the programs work. These programs have trained teachers who are now doing a better job of teaching students, and they created programs customized to their individual needs.

In the introduction to this book, I point out that I have experienced the tremendous boost a culture of coaching provides professional educators. This benefit ultimately transfers to students, who enjoy a heightened passion and skill on the part of their teachers. Coached teachers are fiercely alert to their practice. They reflect on how they achieve learning in their students with other professionals, whose focus and desire is to support them in achieving success.

For those who have not begun, I trust this book has provided you with a framework to incorporate a culture of coaching into your own educational environment. And for those who have coaching programs under way, I hope you have been inspired to continue moving from good to great and to share the benefits of your culture of coaching with as many other educators and administrators as you can.

In short, share the "Wow!"

References

Agnes, M. Editor. (1999). *Webster's new world college dictionary* (4th ed.). Hoboken, N.J.: John Wiley and Sons.

Baker, R. G. (1983). *The contribution of coaching to transfer of training.* Unpublished doctoral dissertation, University of Oregon, Eugene.

Block, P. (1990). *The empowered manager.* San Francisco: Jossey-Bass.

Bowman, C. L., and S. McCormick. (2000). Comparison of peer coaching versus traditional supervision effects. *Journal of Educational Research,* 93(4), 256–262.

Covey, S. (1990). *Seven habits of highly effective people.* New York: Simon and Schuster.

Diamond, J. (1979). *Behavioral kinesiology.* New York: Harper and Row.

Dougherty, D. C. (1993). Peer coaching: Creating a collaborative environment for change. *Dissertation Abstracts International,* 54(1), 71A.

Esquith, R. (2003). *There are no shortcuts: How an inner-city teacher—winner of the American Teacher Award—inspires his students and challenges us to re-think the way we educate our children.* New York: Pantheon Books.

Garmston, R. J. (1987). How administrators support peer coaching. *Educational Leadership* 45(6), 18–27.

Glasser, W. (1992). Quality, trust, and redefining education. *Education Week,* 5/13/92.

Glasser, W. (1998). *The quality school: Managing students without coercion* (3rd ed). New York: HarperCollins.

Glasser, W., and K. L. Dotson. (1998). *Choice theory in the classroom.* New York: HarperCollins.

Goodlad, J. I. (1984). *A place called school.* New York: McGraw-Hill.

Goodlad, J. I. (1994). *Educational renewal: Better teachers, better schools.* San Francisco: Jossey-Bass.

Gordon, W. J. J. (1961). *Synectics.* Cambridge, Mass.: Synectics.

Grinder, J., and R. Bandler. (1981). *Frogs into princes.* Moab, Utah: Real People.

Harriman, S. G. (1992). An evaluative study of teacher portraiture. Doctoral dissertation, University of Connecticut. *Dissertation Abstracts International,* 53(9), 3093A.

Hart, L. A. (1998). *Human brain and human learning.* Kent, Wash.: Books for Educators.

Hasenstab, J. K, S. G. Barkley, and G. M. Flaherty. (1996). *Coaching skills for successful teaching™.* Emerson, N.J.: Performance Learning Systems, Inc.

Heberly, J. (1991). A comparison of the use of the peer-coaching format with the workshop format in changing teacher skills. Doctoral dissertation, University of Idaho. *Dissertation Abstracts International,* 52(7), 2505A.

Jenkins, J., and M. L. Veal. (2002). Preservice teachers' PCK development during peer coaching. *Journal of Teaching in Physical Education,* 22(1), 49–68.

Jensen, E. (1997). *Completing the puzzle: The brain-compatible approach to learning* (2nd ed.). Del Mar, Calif.: Brain Store.

Jensen, E. (1998). *Teaching with the brain in mind.* Alexandria, Va.: ASCD.

Johnson, S. M., and S. M. Kardos. (2002). Keeping new teacher in mind. *Educational Leadership,* 59(6), 13–16.

Joyce B., and B. Showers. (1982). The coaching of teaching. *Educational Leadership,* 40(1), 4–8, 10.

Joyce B., and B. Showers. (1990). *Staff development and student achievement.* White Plains, N.Y.: Longman.

Joyce B., and B. Showers. (2003). *Student achievement through staff development,* 3rd ed. Alexandria, VA: ASCD.

Joyce, B., J. Wolf, and E. Calhoun. (1993). *The self-renewing school.* Alexandria, Va.: ASCD.

Kohler, F. W., K. M. Crilley, D. D. Shearer, and G. Good. (1997). Effects for peer coaching on teacher and student outcomes. *Journal of Educational Research,* 90, 240–250.

Kovalik, S., and K. Olsen. (1997). *ITI: The model: Integrated thematic instruction* (3rd ed.). Kent, Wash.: Books for Educators.

MacLean, P. (1978). A mind of three minds: Educating the triune brain. *77th Yearbook of the National Society for the Study of Education.* Chicago: University of Chicago Press.

Martin, C. (2001). *The life coaching handbook.* Carmarthen, Wales, U.K.: Crown House Publishing, Limited.

McGraw, P. (1999). *Life strategies: Doing what works, doing what matters.* New York: Hyperion.

Mehrabian, A., and M. Weiner. (1967). Decoding of inconsistent communication. *Journal of Personality and Social Psychology,* 6, 109–114.

Morrison, G. M., D. Walker, P. Wakefield, and S. Solberg. (1994). Teacher preferences for collaborative relationships: Relationship to efficacy for teaching prevention-related domains. *Psychology in the Schools,* 31, 221–231.

Peters, T. (1994). *The pursuit of WOW!* New York: Vintage Books.

Philpott, J. S. (1983). *The relative contribution to meaning of verbal and nonverbal channels of communication.* Unpublished master's thesis, University of Nebraska.

Raney, P., and P. Robbins. (1989). Professional growth and support through peer coaching. *Educational Leadership,* 46(8), 35–38. Reproduction Service ED 466 461.

Reese, C. (1986, July 11). A guide for assessing public issues: Remember to do it on four levels. *Orlando Sentinel,* p. A10.

Sadker, D., and M. Sadker. (1985, January). Is the o.k. classroom o.k.? *Phi Delta Kappan.*

Sagor, R. (2003). *Motivating students and teachers in an era of standards.* Alexandria, Va.: ASCD.

Scott, S. (2002). *Fierce conversations: Achieving success at work and in life, one conversation at a time.* New York: Penguin.

Senge, P. M. (1990). *The fifth discipline: The art and practice of the learning organization.* New York: Doubleday/Currency.

Senge, P. M. (1999). *The dance of change: The challenges to sustaining momentum in learning organizations.* New York: Currency/Doubleday.

Showers, B. (1990). Aiming for superior classroom instruction for all children: A comprehensive staff development model. *Remedial and Special Education,* 11(3), 35–39.

Smylie, M. A. (1989). Teachers' views of the effectiveness of sources of learning to teach. *Elementary School Journal,* 89, 543–558.

Storms, B. A., and G. Lee. (2001). *How differences in program implementation influence opportunities for developing reflective practice.* Paper presented at the annual meeting of the American Educational Research Association, Seattle, Washington. (ERIC Document Reproduction Service No. 466 461).

Wheatley, M. (2002). *Turning to one another: Simple conversations to restore hope to the future.* San Francisco: Berrett-Koehler.

Wineburg, M. S. (1995). *The process of peer coaching in the implementation of cooperative learning structures.* Paper presented at the annual meeting of the American Educational Research Association, San Francisco. (ERIC Document Reproduction Service 385528)

Index

About the Author

Stephen G. Barkley is a consultant and educator who serves as executive vice president of Performance Learning Systems, Inc. He has twenty-five years of experience teaching educators and administrators, working with school districts and state departments of education, and providing training in the private sector. Stephen is a riveting and motivational keynote speaker, trainer, and consultant to educators and business people alike.

Having been coached throughout his teaching and consulting career, he has firsthand experience with the personal and professional rewards of collegial coaching relationships.